Lab Manual

to Accompany

Network+ Fundamentals and Certification

Cisco Learning Institute

Russell Hillpot

Michael Ivy

PEARSON

Prentice Hall

Upper Saddle River, New Jersey
Columbus, Ohio

Assistant Vice President and Publisher: Charles E. Stewart, Jr.
Production Editor: Alexandrina Benedicto Wolf
Design Coordinator: Diane Ernsberger
Cover Designer: Jeff Vanik
Cover art: Apart Creations
Production Manager: Matt Ottenweller
Marketing Manager: Ben Leonard

This book was set in Times Roman by *The GTS Companies*/York, PA Campus. It was printed and bound by R.R. Donnelley & Sons Company. The cover was printed by Phoenix Color Corp.

All character names (e.g., Joe Tekk and Ken Koder) are registered trademarks of Prentice Hall.

Linux screen shots © 1999 courtesy of Red Hat, Inc. All rights reserved by Red Hat, Inc. Reprinted with permission.

Microsoft screen captures courtesy of Microsoft, all rights reserved.

NetWare screen shots used with permission from Novell, Inc. Copyright © 2002 Novell, Inc. All rights reserved. NetWare and Novell are registered trademarks of Novell, Inc. in the United States and other countries.

Cisco Learning Institute™ is a trademark of Cisco Learning Institute.

Pearson Education Ltd.
Pearson Education Singapore Pte. Ltd.
Pearson Education Canada, Ltd.
Pearson Education—Japan

Pearson Education Australia Pty. Limited
Pearson Education North Asia Ltd.
Pearson Educación de Mexico, S.A. de C.V.
Pearson Education Malaysia Pte. Ltd.

10 9 8 7 6 5 4 3 2 1
ISBN 0-13-189213-4

Contents

PREFACE   vii

**STATE OF THE INFORMATION TECHNOLOGY
(IT) FIELD**   xi

LAB 1.1   OSI REFERENCE MODEL   1

LAB 1.2   NETWORK+ JOURNAL   3

LAB 1.3   OSI & TCP/IP MODEL EXERCISE   5

LAB 2.1   PHYSICAL NETWORK TOPOLOGY   7

LAB 2.2   MESH TOPOLOGY CHECKUP   9

LAB 2.3   TOPOLOGY COMPARISON   11

LAB 3.1   BUILD A PATCH CABLE (STRAIGHT)   13

LAB 3.2   BUILD A PATCH CABLE (CROSSOVER)   17

LAB 3.3   BUILD A PATCH CABLE (ROLLOVER)   21

**LAB 3.4   NETWORK INTERFACE CARD (NIC)
INSTALLATION**   25

LAB 4.1   DISCOVERING ETHERNET TECHNOLOGIES   29

LAB 4.2   ETHERNET FRAME ANALYZING   31

LAB 4.3   ETHERNET CONNECTOR IDENTIFICATION   33

LAB 5.1   TOKEN RING TROUBLESHOOTING   35

LAB 5.2   TOKEN RING PATHS   37

LAB 6.1   DIRECT CONNECTION FOR TWO COMPUTERS   39

LAB 6.2   CONNECTING TO A REMOTE NETWORK WITH A VPN   43

LAB 6.3   NETWORK UTILITIES/IPCONFIG & PING   45

LAB 7.1   NETSTAT   49

LAB 7.2   NBTSTAT   51

LAB 7.3   NETWORK PROTOCOLS   55

LAB 8.1   ARP & RARP   57

LAB 8.2   IP ADDRESSING PRACTICE   59

LAB 8.3   PING AND TRACERT UTILITIES   63

LAB 9.1   CONFIGURING NOVELL/NETWARE SYSTEMS   67

LAB 9.2   TROUBLESHOOTING IPX/SPX NETWORKS   71

LAB 9.3   NETWARE PROTOCOLS   73

LAB 10.1   SWITCHES VERSUS HUBS   75

LAB 10.2   ROUTER BASICS   79

LAB 10.3   ROUTING PROTOCOLS   85

LAB 11.1 PGP (PRETTY GOOD PRIVACY)   87

LAB 11.2 SOFTWARE FIREWALL   89

LAB 11.3 VIRUS PROTECTION   91

LAB 12.1 E-MAIL CLIENT CONFIGURATION   93

LAB 12.2 ZIPPING E-MAIL ATTACHMENTS   101

LAB 12.3 E-MAIL ANALYSIS   107

LAB 13.1 FTP COMMANDS   109

LAB 13.2 FTP EXPLORER   111

LAB 13.3 FTP FILE TRANSFER USING FTP EXPLORER   115

LAB 14.1 IMAGE FILES   119

LAB 14.2 SOUND FILE COMPARISON   123

LAB 14.3 MULTIMEDIA FILE FORMATS   127

LAB 15.1 BUILDING A WEB PAGE   129

LAB 15.2 WRITING A JAVASCRIPT APPLICATION   135

LAB 15.3 APACHE WEB SERVER   139

LAB 16.1 NETWORK PRINTING   141

LAB 16.2 MAPPING A NETWORK DRIVE   143

LAB 16.3 DIAL-UP NETWORKING   147

LAB 17.1 ROUTING AND REMOTE ACCESS
          SERVICE (RRAS)   151

**LAB 17.2 DYNAMIC HOST CONFIGURATION
PROTOCOL (DHCP)** 153

LAB 17.3 DOMAIN NAME SYSTEM (DNS) 157

LAB 18.1 LINUX DNS SERVICE 159

LAB 18.2 LINUX NIC SETUP 161

LAB 18.3 LINUX NETWORK TESTING 163

LAB 19.1 MAC OS X NETWORKING 169

LAB 19.2 MAC OS X TO WINDOWS XP NETWORKING 171

LAB 19.3 MAC OS X E-MAIL 173

Preface

Computer networks are everywhere. They span the globe, interconnecting with each other, weaving a web of communication that extends outward to the domain of satellites orbiting above the earth. They fail, they heal themselves, and they move staggering amounts of information between distant locations. They are in our schools, our businesses, and even our homes.

The purpose of this textbook is to prepare the reader to successfully prepare for the latest CompTIA Network+ Certification Exam. The attainment of Network+ certification requires that the person seeking certification possess a working knowledge of Network Media and Topologies, Protocols and Standards, Network Implementation, and Network Support. This book is suitable for readers and students in computer engineering technology, electrical engineering technology, networking technology, and telecommunications technology programs, as well as corporations and government agencies.

Concepts and techniques are presented through real-world examples (such as examining all the packets captured while loading a Web page or sending e-mail). Where appropriate, the Internet is used to explain a new network service or mechanism. This includes heavy use of various sites located on the World Wide Web. In Part III, we demonstrate the use of many of the networking concepts covered in Part II in several network client-server applications, Java applets, and CGI programming examples.

■ ORGANIZATION OF THE MAIN TEXT

The main text is divided into four parts.

Part I: Network Hardware

The basics of computer networking are presented, with a quick overview of network protocols and history. Networking hardware, topology, and technology (particularly Ethernet) are covered in detail.

Part II: Network Protocols

Wide coverage is provided on many topics relevant to the typical hardware and software protocols employed in computer networks. These topics include the popular TCP/IP suite of protocols, the mechanics of switching and routing, network management and security, and the IEEE 802 standards.

Part III: Network Applications

The principles of operation behind many everyday networking applications are presented in this part, including e-mail, FTP, streaming audio and video, and the Internet browser.

Part IV: Network Operating Systems

This part covers the networking components of several network operating systems (particularly NT/2000 Server, NetWare, and Mac OS X). The operation of a network domain is examined, as are the details of file and printer sharing, dial-up networking, and setting up a network server.

The chapters in each part all have the same format. Each chapter begins with a list of the **Network+ objectives** that are covered in the chapter. Look for objective icons in the text to indicate where specific Network+ objectives are presented.

Also included at the beginning of each chapter are **performance objectives,** which indicate what new skills and knowledge will be learned in the course of completing the chapter. The instructor will usually administer the requirements of the performance objectives. The text section of each chapter, the heart of the chapter, presents all the information needed to perform the exercises and pass the review quiz. The next section of each chapter contains a **troubleshooting** area. Tips, techniques, and real-world problems and their solutions are presented. Last is the **self-test** section to help the student verify understanding of the material. The self-test is divided into two types of test questions: true/false and multiple choice. Answers to self-test questions are given at the end of the book.

Labs are provided for each chapter in the companion laboratory manual. These labs give the Network+ student an opportunity to practice the concepts taught in the chapter.

Industry tips are provided throughout the book. These tips are written by various network professionals and provide insight into how networks are connected and administered. Many different types of troubleshooting tips and helpful facts are also sprinkled throughout the text. Look for the following icons in the margin to find these hints for quick reference:

A rich set of appendices provides details on numerous network-related topics, including telecommunications technology, Web links, the Ethereal protocol analyzer, Windows NT/2000 fault tolerance, setting up a network repair shop, modems, and the process of becoming network certified.

■ SUPPLEMENTS

Network+ Fundamentals and Certification is supported by the following materials:

- ReviewMaster Tutorial on CD packaged with this text, provides review questions designed to prepare the reader for the Network+ examination.
- Another CD-ROM contains useful example programs and files designed to aid the student in developing and understanding the concepts presented in each part. View the README document (text, Microsoft Word, and HTML formats) to get a detailed description of the companion CD-ROM.
- This laboratory manual accompanies the main text and provides hands-on experiments for each chapter.
- An instructor's manual is available, which contains teaching suggestions, sample syllabi and tests, and other helpful items.

■ ACKNOWLEDGMENTS

We would like to thank our editor, Charles Stewart, and his assistant, Maria Rego, for their encouragement and assistance during the development of this project. Thanks also go to our production editor, Alex Wolf, our development editor, Susan Hobbs, and our copyeditor, Bret Workman.

Many individuals and companies have provided permission for their hardware and/or software products, and we appreciate their support:

- Sue Runfola, for screen shot(s) reprinted by permission from Apple Computer, Inc.
- Mariana Mihaylova of Ipswitch, Inc., for screen shots of WS_FTP.
- Christine Kizer of Quantum Corporation, for permission to use photographs of Quantum's Snap Server line of storage solutions, and for her donation of a 40 GB Snap Server 1100 for educational experimentation.
- Sue Goodwill of Novell, Inc.
- Victor Kunkel of TrueTime, Inc., for screen shots of WinSync.
- Corel Corporation for screen shots of HoTMetaL.

State of the Information Technology (IT) Field

Just about all organizations today rely on computers and information technology to streamline business processes and boost productivity and efficiency. Evolving technology further changes how companies do business. The widespread availability of the Internet provides the opportunity for a business to extend its reach around the globe, interacting with customers and suppliers that they were unable to reach before. This fundamental change in business practices has increased the need for skilled and certified IT workers across industries. This shift moves many IT workers out of traditional IT business settings and into many IT-reliant industries such as government, healthcare, insurance, and banking.

According to the U.S. Department of Labor's Bureau of Labor Statistics, in 2000 there were 2.1 million computer and data processing services jobs within organizations and an additional 164,000 self-employed workers. This huge growth in jobs over the last decade has made IT-related jobs one of the largest sectors in the economy. Even in more challenging economic times the job opportunities for skilled and certified IT professionals remain fairly strong.

As with any industry, the workforce is essential in moving business forward. Thanks to evolving technologies, businesses are constantly challenged to keep the IT skills of their workers current. It has been estimated that technologies change approximately every 2 years. With such a short product life cycle employees must strive to keep up with these changes to continually bring value to their employers.

■ CERTIFICATIONS

Many jobs in the IT industry require different levels of education. The level of education and type of training required vary from employer to employer, but the need for qualified workers with verifiable technology skills is a constant. As technology evolves and the number of devices and systems continues to grow, many employers look for employees who possess the skills necessary to implement the latest technology solutions in their companies. One dilemma faced by employers is that traditional degrees and diplomas alone do not identify the precise skills that an applicant possesses. As the IT industry has grown, it has increasingly relied on technical certifications to identify the skills of a particular job applicant. Technical certifications provide an excellent method for employers to ensure the quality and skill qualifications of their computer professionals and can offer job seekers a competitive edge. According to Thomas Regional Industrial Market Trends, one of the 15 trends that will transform the workplace over the next decade is a severe labor and skill shortage, specifically in technical fields, which are struggling to locate skilled and educated workers.

Certifications can be divided into two categories, vendor-neutral and vendor-specific. Vendor-neutral certifications are those that do not subscribe to the technology solutions of a specific vendor, but rather measure the skills and knowledge required in specific industry job roles. Vendor-neutral certifications include all of the Computing Technology Industry Association's (CompTIA) certifications, Project Management Institute's certifications, and Security Certified Program certifications.

Vendor-specific certifications validate the skills and knowledge necessary to be successful utilizing the technology solution of a specific vendor. Some examples of vendor-specific certifications include those offered by Microsoft, IBM, Novell, and Cisco.

In many careers, compensation is determined not only by experience and education, but also by the number and type of certifications earned. As employers grapple to fill open IT positions with qualified candidates, certifications provide a means for employers to validate the skill sets necessary to be successful within their organizations. According to the Department of Labor's Bureau of Labor Statistics, the computer and data processing industry has grown at a dramatic rate from 1990 to 2000 and is anticipated to grow an additional 86% in wages and salaries by the year 2010. Robert Half International reported that starting salaries for help-desk support staff in 2001 ranged from $30,500 to $56,000 and more senior technical support salaries ranged from $48,000 to $61,000 in the United States.

Certification credentials can benefit individuals with more than just a competitive edge over non-certified individuals applying for the IT positions. Some institutions of higher education grant college credit to students who have successfully passed certification exams. Certified individuals are able to move through their degree programs more quickly and they also save money that would have been spent on tuition and books. Many technology certifications give individuals the ability to advance more quickly within the U.S. military. Finally, several advanced certification programs require or accept many certifications as part of their exams. For example, Cisco and Microsoft accept some CompTIA certifications as electives for their certification programs.

■ CAREER PLANNING

Finding a career that fits your personality, skill set, and lifestyle is challenging, fulfilling, and often difficult. What are the steps you should take to find that dream career? First, you wouldn't be reading this unless you had already expressed an interest in IT. The world of work within the IT industry is vast. Are you a person who likes to work alone or do you need to have people around you? Do you like speaking directly with customers or prefer to stay behind the scenes? Does your lifestyle embrace a lot of travel or do you prefer to stay in one location? All of these factors influence an individual's decision when faced with choosing the right job. A first step to learning more about yourself, your interests, work values, and abilities can be obtained by inventory assessments. There are a variety of Web sites that offer assistance with career planning and offer assessments.

The Computing Technology Industry Association (CompTIA) hosts an informational Web site outlining careers in the IT industry called the TechCareer Compass™ (TCC). The TCC is located at http://tcc.comptia.org. This Web site was created by the industry and contains a wealth of information about IT industry jobs. Each job listing includes a description, alternate job titles, critical work functions, activities and performance indicators, and skills and knowledge required by the job. In other words, it shows exactly what the job functions are so that you can find a job that best fits your interests and abilities. Additionally, the TCC maps the objectives of over 700 technical certifications to the skills required by each specific job, allowing individuals to research their job interest, then plan their certification training. Within this Web site is a regularly updated resource section with articles and links to many other career Web sites, which gives an individual a one-stop location for all their IT career information.

In addition to CompTIA's TechCareer Compass, there are many other Web sites that cover components of IT careers and career planning. Many of these sites are listed on the TCC Web site in the Resources section under Career Links. Some of these include YourIT-Future.com, ITCompass.net, and About.com.

As you begin your studies in this text, keep in mind the various resources that are available to you to help plan your career. Your instructor may be able to provide guidance and advice about careers in your local area. Arrange visits with companies. Periodically revisit those that interest you to learn more about potential careers. If possible, arrange an internship to acquire practical skills and experience. Finally, periodically revisit the

TechCareer Compass site to verify that you are on course and moving toward the goals you have set for yourself.

Good luck in this course and in your career.

■ REFERENCES

Bureau of Labor Statistics, U.S. Department of Labor, Career Guide to Industries, 2002–03 Edition, Computer and Data Processing Services, at http://www.bls.gov/oco/cg/cgs033.htm (visited August 14, 2003).

Bureau of Labor Statistics, U.S. Department of Labor, Occupational Outlook Handbook, 2002–03 Edition, Computer Support Specialists and System Administrators, at http://www.bls.gov/oco/home.htm (visited August 14, 2003).

Thomas Regional Industrial Market Trends, July 8, 2003 Newsletter, *15 Trends That Will Transform the Workforce*, at http://www.thomasregional.com/newsarchive2.html?us= 3f61ed4162269&to=5&from=0&id=1057266649 (visited September 10, 2003).

OSI Reference Model

■ INTRODUCTION

This lab will help to reinforce the functions, protocols, mnemonic names, PDUs, and standards of the OSI model. You will use the OSI model throughout your networking career to design and troubleshoot networks. The OSI model may seem rather boring and abstract in the beginning of your Network+ training. Don't skip over this exercise. The OSI model is an integral part of your training.

■ WHAT YOU WILL DO

- Name the seven OSI model layers
- List as many of the PDU's, functions, protocols, etc. from memory as you can. Use the illustrations and text in the book to help. List the media types in the appropriate layers.
- Copy this lab and fill in the appropriate information in each block as many times as it takes to familiarize yourself with the OSI model

Layer	Name	Protocol Data Unit	Primary Functions (key terms)	Protocols	Mnemonic
7					
6					
5					
4					
3					
2					
1					

Network+ Journal

■ INTRODUCTION

This lab will provide you with a valuable tool to document your progress as a network professional.

The practice of documenting steps taken in successful troubleshooting, installation techniques, driver updates, or any other task performed related to your Network+ career is a great habit to develop. How many times have you found yourself in a troubleshooting situation that you faced months ago and could not remember what you did to correct the problem?

An instructor of mine used to say that the three most important things to do regarding building, designing, or troubleshooting networks are to Document, Document, and Document. This is the most important facet of networking that is most often neglected.

■ WHAT YOU WILL DO

- Retain a copy of each lab activity that you complete
- Gather related white papers from reliable sources
- Document troubleshooting steps
- Record your thoughts on each lab experience

■ WHAT YOU WILL NEED

- Network+ textbook and online curriculum
- Labs from each chapter
- 3″ binder
- Tabs to organize the journal

■ STEPS TO COMPLETE

Step 1: Purchase a binder at least 3″ thick.

Step 2: Complete the labs at the end of each chapter of the Network+ curriculum.

Step 3: Place the lab documents in the journal separated by tabs identifying the chapter and exercise performed.

Step 4: Record your thoughts related to the lab and place other pertinent material in the journal with the lab.

OSI & TCP/IP Model Exercise

LAB 1.3

■ STEPS TO COMPLETE

Step 1: Write the OSI or TCP/IP layer number in the blank provided for each of the following network devices, standards, and protocols. Use the index in the text to find references to these terms. Perform an Internet search on the terms and keep your findings in a networking journal.

Step 2: Put this document in your networking journal and add the layer numbers as you learn them.

___ Network	___ Network Access	___ Session
___ Internet (TCP/IP)	___ Presentation	___ Transport
___ Data Link	___ Physical	___ Application
___ Application(TCP/IP)	___ IP	___ UDP
___ HTTP	___ Router	___ Switch
___ Segments	___ Packets	___ UTP
___ CSMA/CD	___ Logical address	___ JPEG
___ Sessions	___ Application (OSI)	___ Data
___ Ethernet address	___ Network layer (TCP/IP)	___ Coax
___ Network topology	___ Inter-host communication	___ Token
___ Access control byte	___ FF:FF:FF:FF:FF:FF	___ IPX
___ TFTP	___ 32-bit address	___ Crosstalk
___ EMI/RFI	___ Network segmentation	___ Voltage
___ PICT	___ Sequencing of segments	___ MPEG
___ TIFF	___ MIDI	___ Telnet
___ TCP	___ DNS	___ Hub
___ Repeater	___ RJ-45	___ Frames
___ Bits	___ 802.2	___ MAC address
___ Physical address	___ ASCII	___ EBCDIC
___ Virtual circuits	___ Path selection	___ Fiber
___ Bridge	___ Data stream	___ CRC
___ 255.255.255.255	___ Flat addressing scheme	___ ARP
___ 4-byte address	___ Acknowledgements	___ Tip and Ring
___ Cancellation	___ Reflection	___ NEXT
___ Data encryption	___ SQL	___ Windowing
___ Cloud	___ Patch panel	___ NFS
___ RPC	___ Compression	___ 6-byte address

Physical Network Topology

■ STEPS TO COMPLETE

Step 1: Draw a diagram of each type of topology.

Step 2: List the advantages/disadvantages of each.

Step 3: Name the type of logical topology used with each physical topology.

A. Bus

B. Star

C. Ring

D. Mesh

E. Hybrid topology

Mesh Topology Checkup

■ STEPS TO COMPLETE

Step 1: Complete the following drawings by drawing the Ethernet links between hosts, providing a mesh topology in each case.

Step 2: Calculate the number of links needed for each network using the following formula:

$$L = N(N - 1)/2$$

Step 3: Do the number of links drawn agree with the number that you calculated? Can you see how the addition of a couple of hosts exponentially increases the number of links needed to implement a full mesh network? How could this affect installation cost? Could this topology type adversely affect troubleshooting efforts?

FIGURE 2.2.1

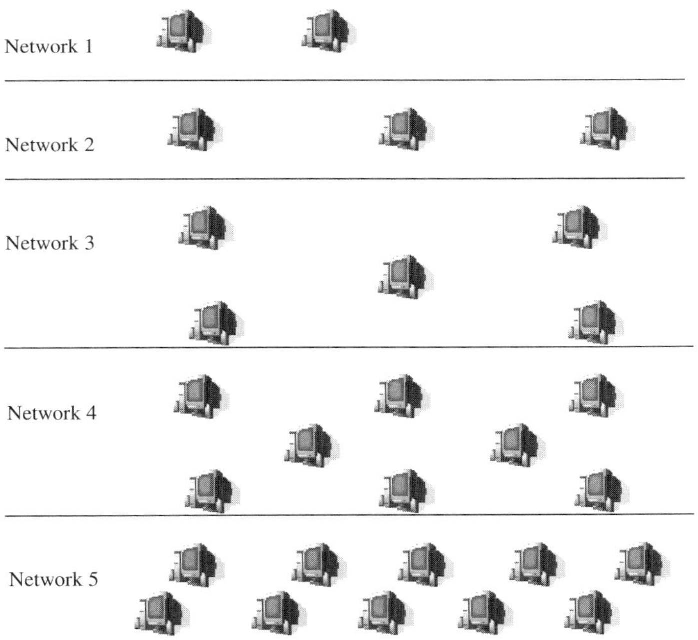

Network 1

Network 2

Network 3

Network 4

Network 5

Topology Comparison

LAB **2.3**

■ STEPS TO COMPLETE

Step 1: Draw a bus, star, ring, and mesh network between the hosts shown.

Step 2: Compare the number of links needed for each topology.

FIGURE 2.3.1

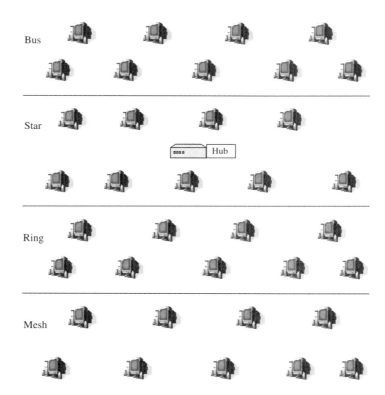

Build a Patch Cable (Straight)

LAB **3.1**

■ INTRODUCTION

Computers, routers, switches, and hubs are among the devices that require the use of a straight cable. This cable is also referred to as a patch cord. The Network+ candidate must be able to recognize the various cables used to connect network equipment by observing the wiring standard used in the RJ-45 cable connector.

Some cables may be manufactured using unorthodox wiring methods. The Network+ candidate must be able to discern which configuration the cabling terminated in the connector represents.

The process of building various cable types reinforces proper cabling standards. The standards used for Ethernet cabling are TIA/EIA 568A and TIA/EIA 568B. The 568B standard is more commonly used with business and industrial cabling. The HTI+ curriculum states that the 568A standard is specified for use in home Ethernet installations. Network technicians do not change the whole network if it is wired to a standard other than what is required for new installations. They simply match the existing standard used for the local network. After all, the network technician is most often limited by the customer budget. If it isn't broken, most network administrators will not fix it.

■ WHAT YOU WILL DO

- Build an Ethernet cable
- Visually inspect the cable
- Test the cable with a cable tester

■ WHAT YOU WILL NEED

- RJ-45 continuity tester
- 3–5 meters of CAT 5e UTP cable
- RJ-45 connectors
- Crimping tool with RJ-45 die
- UTP wire strippers
- Wire pliers
- Knife

■ SETTING UP

Make sure you have all the tools and materials stated above. The assistance of an experienced teacher cannot be overemphasized. It may be helpful to find an experienced network technician that will allow you to observe cable building.

Part I Build the Cable

1. Cut the UTP to the desired length. Consider color coding wires in relation to type (i.e., red for straight, blue for crossover, etc.).

2. Use the wire strippers to cut the UTP cable jacket a couple inches from the end. Circle the stripper around the cable only one time to avoid cutting the inner strands of UTP.

3. Remove the jacket.

4. Cut the reinforcement filament even with the end of the jacket with your knife or scissors.

5. Inspect the wires to make sure that the insulation was not nicked during the stripping process.

6. Untwist each pair of wires back to the point where the jacket was removed, but no further than that.

7. Straighten out each pair of wires as much as possible while holding the jacket where it was cut and arrange them in the order in which they will be placed in the RJ-45 connector. The wiring standard used for typical office and business applications is EIA/TIA 568B. EIA/TIA 568B requires the wires to be arranged in the RJ-45 jack as follows, viewing the jack from the open end with the clip facing down, left to right: orange/white, orange, green/white, blue, blue/white, green, brown/white, brown.

8. Various methods can be used to organize the wires in the proper order. Some technicians find it easier to untwist the green and blue pairs first and arrange them in order since the green pair must be split. Whatever works for you is great as long as the wire is not untwisted back into the jacket. Maintain as much of the twist as possible and build the cable right in order to prevent the effects of NEXT (Near-end Crosstalk).

9. The wires should be cut in a straight line about ½″ to ¾″ from the end for the jacket. The RJ-45 jack can be used to measure the approximate length by holding it next to the cable and cutting it to the proper length. Look at the RJ-45 jack and observe that the design of the jack steps up about ½″ from the end. Mark the spot to cut the wire with your thumb and cut the wires evenly. Another possible method is to put a mark on the work bench as a ½″ template and use it to measure the cutting point. It is also very important to have a cutting tool that cuts straight across and is sharp enough to cut cleanly.

10. Place the wires into the RJ-45 connector, making sure that the proper wire color order is maintained. Slide the wires firmly into the connector and observe that each strand butts to the end of the connector. The copper ends of the wires should be visible at the end of the jack. If the former steps were performed properly, the jacket end should be pressed inside the connector far enough that the jacket is held by the crimp mechanism of the RJ-45 connector when crimped.

11. Slide the connector into the crimping tool while holding the jacket in place. Crimp the cable and make sure that the jacket is effectively crimped so as to provide strain relief to the connection. Some crimping tools are ratcheting type and will release only when the full crimp has been accomplished. These are the best tools to use when several cables have to be made.

12. Repeat steps 2–11 for the other end of the cable.

13. Both ends of the cable are wired exactly the same to make a straight cable.

Part 2 Test the Cable

1. Test the cable with a cable tester. If the cable test indicates a good cable, proceed to the next step. If not, start the process over on the faulty end. (Note: A good quality tester can determine the location and type of fault.)

Part 3 Label the Cable

1. Label the cable as straight and note the length. A name designating the location or a cable number may also be included on the label.

FIGURE 3.1.1

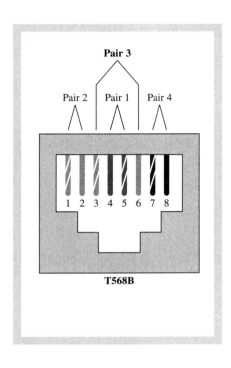

Build a Patch Cable (Crossover)

■ INTRODUCTION

Computers, routers, switches, and hubs are among the devices that require the use of a crossover cable. A crossover cable is used to connect two computers directly together. It is also used to connect two hubs together if an uplink port is not available on the hub. You can also use a crossover to connect two switches together.

The crossover cable is constructed with the transmit and receive pairs reversed on each end of the cable.

Some cables may be manufactured using unorthodox wiring methods. The Network+ candidate must be able to discern which configuration the cabling terminated in the connector represents.

The process of building various cable types reinforces proper cabling standards. The standards used for Ethernet cabling are TIA/EIA 568A and TIA/EIA 568B. The 568B standard is more commonly used with business and industrial cabling. The crossover cable is built using the 568A standard on one connector and the 568B standard on the connector on the other end of the cable.

■ WHAT YOU WILL DO

- Build a crossover Ethernet cable
- Visually inspect the cable
- Test the cable with a cable tester

■ WHAT YOU WILL NEED

- RJ-45 continuity tester
- 3–5 meters of CAT 5e UTP cable
- RJ-45 connectors
- Crimping tool with RJ-45 die
- UTP wire strippers
- Wire pliers
- Knife

■ SETTING UP

Make sure you have all the tools and materials stated above. The assistance of an experienced teacher cannot be overemphasized. It may be helpful to find an experienced network technician that will allow you to observe cable building.

Part I Build the Cable

1. Cut the UTP to the desired length. Consider color coding wires in relation to type (i.e., red for straight, blue for crossover, etc.).

2. Use the wire strippers to cut the UTP cable jacket a couple inches from the end. Circle the stripper around the cable only one time to avoid cutting the inner strands of UTP.

3. Remove the jacket.

4. Cut the reinforcement filament even with the end of the jacket with your knife or scissors.

5. Inspect the wires to make sure that the insulation was not nicked during the stripping process.

6. Untwist each pair of wires back to the point where the jacket was removed.

7. Straighten out each pair of wires as much as possible while holding the jacket where it was cut and arrange the wires in the order in which they will be placed in the RJ-45 connector. The wiring standard used for typical office and business applications is EIA/TIA 568B. EIA/TIA 568B requires the wires to be arranged in the RJ-45 jack as follows, viewing the jack from the open end with the clip facing down, left to right: orange/white, orange, green/white, blue, blue/white, green, brown/white, brown. The RJ-45 connector on the other end of the cable will be terminated according to the EIA/TIA 568A standard. That standard is as follows, viewing the jack from the open end with the clip facing down, left to right: green/white, green, orange/white, blue, blue/white, orange, brown/white, brown.

8. There are various methods that can be used to organize the wires in the proper order. Some find it easier to untwist the green and blue pairs first and arrange them in order since the green pair must be split. Whatever works for you is great as long as the wire is not untwisted back into the jacket. Maintain as much of the twist as possible and build the cable right in order to prevent the effects of NEXT.

9. The wires should be cut in a straight line about ½″ to ¾″ from the end for the jacket. The RJ-45 jack can be used to measure the approximate length by holding it next to the cable and cutting it to the proper length. Look at the RJ-45 jack and observe that the design of the jack steps up about ½″ from the end. Mark the spot to cut the wire with your thumb and cut the wires evenly. Another possible method is to put a mark on the work bench as a ½″ template and use it to measure the cutting point. It is also very important to have a cutting tool that cuts straight across and is sharp enough to cut cleanly.

10. Place the wires into the RJ-45 connector, making sure that the proper wire color order is maintained. Slide the wires firmly into the connector and observe that each strand butts to the end of the connector. The copper ends of the wires should be visible at the end of the jack. If the former steps were performed properly, the jacket end should be pressed inside the connector far enough that the jacket is held by the crimp mechanism of the RJ-45 connector when crimped.

11. Slide the connector into the crimping tool while holding the jacket in place. Crimp the cable and make sure that the jacket is effectively crimped so as to provide strain relief to the connection. Some crimping tools are ratcheting type and will release only when the full crimp has been accomplished. These are the best tools to use when several cables have to be made.

12. Repeat steps 2–11 for the other end of the cable with one exception: This end of the cable should be wired to the TIA/EIA 568A standard. The TIA/EIA 568A standard requires that the wires be arranged in the RJ-45 jack as follows, viewing the jack from the open end with the clip facing down, left to right: green/white, green, orange/white, blue, blue/white, orange, brown/white, brown.

13. Simply stated, the 1&2 and 3&6 position wires will swap positions on each end to make a crossover cable.

Part 2 Test the Cable

1. Test the cable with a cable tester. If the cable tests good, proceed to the next step. If not, start the process over on the faulty end. (Note: A good quality tester can determine the location and type of fault. The cable tester will most likely indicate a miswire when testing a crossover cable. The test should indicate no opens or shorts and that the 1&2 and 3&6 cables are crossed. You must know which wires should be different on each end. Remember that the green pair and the orange pair are the only pairs affected by the cross.)

Part 3 Label the Cable

1. Label the cable as a crossover and note the length. A name designating the location or a cable number may also be included on the label.

FIGURE 3.2.1

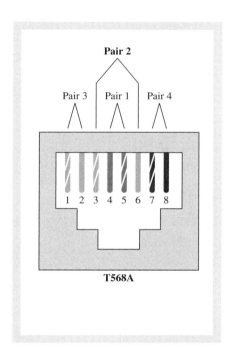 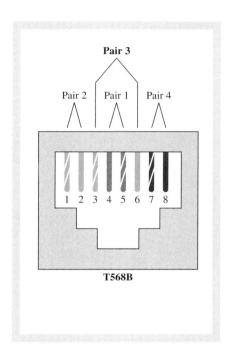

Build a Patch Cable (Rollover)

LAB **3.3**

■ INTRODUCTION

Computers, routers, and switches are among the devices that require the use of a rollover cable. A rollover cable is used to connect a workstation or dumb terminal to the console port on the back of a router or switch.

The rollover cable is used from an asynchronous serial interface to the console port of a router or switch. The settings made on the computer's COM port should be set to 8 data bits, no parity, and 2 stop bits.

Each end of the rollover cable has an RJ-45 connector. The wiring scheme on each end of the cable is exactly the opposite of that of the other end. When the cable is completed and tested, it can be used to establish a console connection with a router or switch using terminal emulation software such as HyperTerminal.

The end connected to the computer plugs into an RJ-45 to DB9 terminal adapter, and the other end plugs directly into the RJ-45 console port on the router or switch.

Some cables may be manufactured using unorthodox wiring methods. The Network+ candidate must be able to discern which configuration the cabling terminated in the connector represents.

The process of building various cable types reinforces proper cabling standards. The standards used for Ethernet cabling are TIA/EIA 568A and TIA/EIA 568B. The 568B standard is more commonly used with business and industrial cabling. The rollover cable is built using the 568B standard on one connector and the exact opposite of the 568B standard on the connector on the other end of the cable.

■ WHAT YOU WILL DO

- Build a rollover console cable
- Visually inspect the cable
- Test the cable with a cable tester

■ WHAT YOU WILL NEED

- RJ-45 continuity tester
- 3–5 meters of CAT 5e UTP cable
- RJ-45 connectors
- Crimping tool with RJ-45 die
- UTP wire strippers
- Wire pliers
- Knife

■ SETTING UP

Make sure you have all the tools and materials stated above. The assistance of an experienced teacher cannot be overemphasized. It may be helpful to find an experienced network technician that will allow you to observe cable building.

Part I Build the Cable

1. Cut the UTP to the desired length. Consider color coding wires in relation to type (i.e., red for straight, blue for crossover, etc.).

2. Use the wire strippers to cut the UTP cable jacket a couple inches from the end. Circle the stripper around the cable only one time to avoid cutting the inner strands of UTP.

3. Remove the jacket.

4. Cut the reinforcement material even with the end of the jacket with your knife or scissors.

5. Inspect the wires to make sure that the insulation was not nicked during the stripping process.

6. Untwist each pair of wires back to the point where the jacket was removed.

7. Straighten out each pair of wires as much as possible while holding the jacket where it was cut and arrange the wires in the order in which they will be placed in the RJ-45 connector. The wiring standard used for typical office and business applications is EIA/TIA 568B. EIA/TIA 568B requires the wires to be arranged in the RJ-45 jack as follows, viewing the jack from the open end with the clip facing down, left to right: orange/white, orange, green/white, blue, blue/white, green, brown/white, brown. The RJ-45 connector on the other end of the cable will be terminated exactly opposite to the EIA/TIA 568B standard. Complete this end. The easiest method to facilitate the process of building the other end will be explained later.

8. Various methods can be used to organize the wires in the proper order. Some find it easier to untwist the green and blue pairs first and arrange them in order since the green pair must be split. Whatever works for you is great as long as the wire is not untwisted back into the jacket. Maintain as much of the twist as possible and build the cable right in order to prevent the effects of NEXT.

9. The wires should be cut in a straight line about ½″ to ¾″ from the end for the jacket. The RJ-45 jack can be used to measure the approximate length by holding it next to the cable and cutting it to the proper length. Look at the RJ-45 jack and observe that the design of the jack steps up about ½″ from the end. Mark the spot to cut the wire with your thumb and cut the wires evenly. Another possible method is to put a mark on the work bench as a ½″ template and use it to measure the cutting point. It is also very important to have a cutting tool that cuts straight across and is sharp enough to cut cleanly.

10. Place the wires into the RJ-45 connector, making sure that the proper wire color order is maintained. Slide the wires firmly into the connector and observe that each strand butts to the end of the connector. The copper ends of the wires should be visible at the end of the jack. If the former steps were performed properly, the jacket end should be pressed inside the connector far enough that the jacket is held by the crimp mechanism of the RJ-45 connector when crimped.

11. Slide the connector into the crimping tool while holding the jacket in place. Crimp the cable and make sure that the jacket is effectively crimped so as to provide strain relief to the connection. Some crimping tools are ratcheting type and will release only when the full crimp has been accomplished. These are the best tools to use when several cables have to be made.

12. Repeat steps 2–11 for the other end of the cable with one exception: Arrange the wires according to the TIA/EIA 568B standard. Now rotate the position of the RJ-45 jack so that the clip is facing up. Slide the wires into the connector following the method prescribed in steps 2–11 and note that each end of the cable is wired exactly opposite the other end.

13. Simply stated, all of the wires will be opposite on each end to make a rollover cable.

Part 2 Test the Cable

1. Test the cable with a cable tester. If the cable tests good, proceed to the next step. If not, start the process over on the faulty end. (Note: A good quality tester can determine the location and type of fault. The cable tester will most likely indicate a miswire when testing a rollover cable. The test should indicate no opens or shorts and that the wires 1 through 8 are terminated exactly opposite. You must know which wires should be different on each end.

Part 3 Label the Cable

1. Label the cable as a rollover and note the length. A name designating the location or a cable number may also be included on the label.

FIGURE 3.3.1

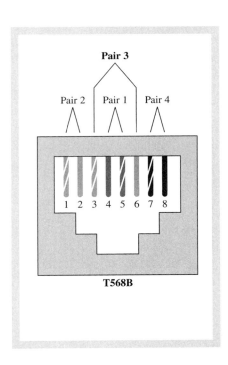

Network Interface Card (NIC) Installation

LAB **3.4**

■ INTRODUCTION

The installation of a NIC facilitates the connection of a computer to a network. This connection permits the connected computer to participate in a network and all this entails. Files, printers, scanners, and virtually any other device connected to any other computer on the network can be shared.

The definition of a network is two or more computers connected in order to communicate, share files, and other resources.

The NIC can be thought of as the interface to the network.

■ WHAT YOU WILL DO

- Check a NIC for compatibility using the Hardware Compatibility List (HCL) for the Windows 2000 operating system used in the computer
- Install a NIC in a computer
- Connect proper cables to another NIC-equipped computer
- Configure the IP address, subnet mask, and default gateway

■ WHAT YOU WILL NEED

- Computer with Windows 2000 installed
- NIC compatible with the operating system used
- Phillips screwdriver
- Straight cable to connect to hub, or crossover cable to connect directly to another computer

■ SETTING UP

Make sure you have all the tools and materials stated above. The assistance of an experienced teacher cannot be overemphasized. It may be helpful to find an experienced network technician that will allow you to observe NIC installation. Experienced technicians may be able to offer insight related to buying cards that will install with ease. Following directions cannot be overemphasized. The HCL is a valuable tool to explore in order to avoid difficulties associated with NICs that may not be compatible with the operating system used. The Internet is a valuable source for information related to the best NICs to purchase for a particular system. Chat rooms related to NIC installation problems for particular operating systems are available.

Part 1 Check NIC for Compatibility with Operating System

1. Check the NIC packaging for information on use with your particular operating system. The instruction in this lab pertains specifically to Windows 2000 operations systems.

2. The type of expansion slots available on your computer will determine your selection of a NIC. PCI slots are typically used for NIC installation in modern computers, but other types of expansion slots can be used.

3. The HCL should be consulted on the operating system manufacturer's web site.

4. NIC card manufacturer web sites related to available drivers can also be consulted even though most approved NICs come with a disk with the applicable drivers or Windows 2000 will have the needed drivers.

Part 2 NIC Installation

1. Turn off the power to the computer.

2. Unplug the computer and press the power switch to eliminate any possibility of residual voltage.

3. Remove the computer cover.

4. Put an ESD ground wrist strap on and clip it to an unpainted part of the computer framework.

5. Decide which slot you wish to install the NIC in. If there is room, it is often a good idea to leave a space between installed cards. This space makes it easier to install and remove the cables from the NIC.

6. Remove the slot cover by removing the screw that holds it in place. Retain the screw.

7. Remove the NIC from the static packaging. Try to handle the NIC with the fingertips on the sides of the upper portion of the card. Avoid touching the part of the card that inserts into the PCI slot or any of the chips located on the card.

8. Position the NIC over the PCI bus that is aligned with the removed slot cover.

9. Install the NIC into the slot with a gentle rocking motion. Make sure all the pins of the card properly align with the selected slot. Press the card down into the slot and install the screw retained from step 6.

10. Reinstall the computer cover and the power cord.

11. Boot up the computer.

12. The New Hardware Detected dialog box may ask that you insert your Windows 2000 CD. If a suitable driver cannot be found, it may ask for the disk that came with the card. If you have to use this option, insert the disk and choose *Browse*. Locate the folder named *Windows 2000*, *W2k*, and so on. Click *OK*.

13. Windows 2000 will automatically configure and use the card after it has installed the software for it.

14. Check Device Manager to make sure that there are no yellow exclamation mark icons to the left of the card name. The card name should appear without any troubling icons.

Part 3

1. Plug a crossover cable into the NIC port of each computer.

2. A straight cable may be used if a hub is used to connect the two computers.

Part 4

1. Click *Start*, *Settings*, *Network and Dial-Up Connections*. Choose Local Area Connection and select *Properties*. A Properties dialog box with your network card named should appear under Connect Using.

2. Click Install, and from the list choose a Network Component Type. Click *Client* and then *Add*.

3. From the list of network clients, choose *Client for Microsoft Networks* and *OK*. Insert the Windows 2000 disk if asked.

4. To share files, printers, and so on click *Service*, *Add*, *File and Printer Sharing for Microsoft Networks*, and *OK*. A check mark should appear next to File and Printer Sharing.

5. Under the Protocols heading, select *Internet Protocol (TCP/IP)*. Add it. Add NetBEUI if you have Windows 98 computers without TCP/IP.

6. In *Local Area Connections Properties*, select *Internet Protocol (TCP/IP)*. Click *Properties*.

7. Click *Use the following IP address*.

8. For a two-computer connection, use the following settings. (If you are connecting to an existing LAN, the network settings used must agree with the existing network)

9. On one computer, choose an IP address of 10.0.1.1, a subnet mask of 255.255.255.0, and a default gateway of 10.0.1.254. On the other computer change the IP address setting to 10.0.1.2 and use the same subnet mask and default gateway settings.

10. Right-click *My Computer* and choose *Properties*. Click *Network Identification*. Does each computer have a different computer name and the same workgroup name? If not, choose the Network ID and follow the wizard to configure this. Click *This computer is for home use and not part of a business network*. Next, enter a name for your workgroup. Click *Next* and finish by rebooting your computer. The same workgroup name must be used on each computer connected if files and printers are shared.

Discovering Ethernet Technologies

■ INTRODUCTION

The knowledge of various Ethernet technologies is vital to the Network+ candidate. The prepared network technician understands the limitations of the technology in use. This lab explores the various technologies, revealing the cable, speed, signaling method, distance, and topology used for each specific Ethernet technology.

An understanding of how each Ethernet technology operates also assists the network technician in troubleshooting network problems.

■ WHAT YOU WILL DO

- Research the different Ethernet technologies listed in this lab
- Complete a chart related to the various Ethernet technologies

■ WHAT YOU WILL NEED

- Network+ book
- Chart

■ SETTING UP

Familiarize yourself with the various cables used to connect the various technologies. Inspect the various types of cable, if possible. A picture of the cable types can be used if physical access to cabling is not possible. Complete the chart from memory as much as possible after reading the chapter. Use the curriculum book to fill in the blanks remaining.

Part I Research Ethernet Technologies

1. Study the various Ethernet technologies using the curriculum book and any other reliable source. Do an Internet search.

Part 2 Complete the Chart

1. Complete as much of the following chart as possible from memory.

2. Use the curriculum book or your outside research material to finish the chart.

3. Place the chart in your journal.

Ethernet Type	Media Used	Impedance	Connector Used	Segment Length	Maximum Hosts/ Segment	Distance Between Hosts	Topology
10BASE5							
10BASE2							
10BASE-T							
10BASE-FL							
10BASE-FB							
10BASE-FP							
100BASE-T4							
100BASE-TX							
100BASE-FX							
1000BASE-T							
1000BASE-CX							
1000BASE-SX							
1000BASE-LX							

Ethernet Frame Analyzing

■ INTRODUCTION

The knowledge of various Ethernet technologies is vital to the Network+ candidate. The prepared network technician understands the limitations of the technology in use. This chapter explores the various technologies, revealing the cable, speed, signaling method, distance, and topology used for each specific Ethernet technology.

An understanding of how each Ethernet technology operates also assists the network technician in troubleshooting network problems.

A packet sniffer is a useful tool for the beginner or veteran Network+ practitioner. A packet sniffer enables the network technician to see what traffic is traversing the network. Packet sniffers provide us with the ability to see the frames on the wire and decode the 1's and 0's.

The purpose of a packet sniffer in this chapter is to expose the Network+ student to Ethernet frames. The ability to visually experience the transmission of Ethernet frames across a network and decode them for content helps the Network+ student understand how frames are transmitted across a network segment.

You must get permission to use a packet sniffer or protocol analyzer on any network segment to which you have access. An Internet search for packet sniffers will reveal several to try out. Appendix F of the text provides information about a protocol analyzer called Ethereal.

■ WHAT YOU WILL DO

- Obtain permission to use a packet sniffer or protocol analyzer on a network segment
- Internet search for trial use of a packet sniffer or analyzer
- Install the packet sniffer or protocol analyzer
- Follow instructions related to the software
- Examine packets and frames

■ WHAT YOU WILL NEED

- Access to network segment or lab
- Permission from network administrator
- Packet sniffer or protocol analyzer

■ SETTING UP

Part 1 Obtain Permission from Network Administrator

1. Ask for permission to use the sniffer or analyzer.

Part 2 Internet Search

1. A word search for "packet sniffers" should be sufficient to find one suitable for the purposes of this lab.

Part 3 Packet Sniffer Installation

1. Install the software according to the directions provided.

Part 4 Start the Sniffer

1. Examine frames and packets while performing Internet searches.

2. Observe all aspects of the Ethernet frame:
   A. MAC addressing
   B. IP address
   C. Content decoding

3. Capture and copy output for future examination.

4. Place the lab in your journal.

Ethernet Connector Identification

■ INTRODUCTION

The Network+ technician must be able to identify the various cables, connectors, and interface types. The ability to identify and use the proper cable and connector is a necessity. An identifying mark of experience and professionalism is the ability to recognize and connect the various types of network connectors.

■ WHAT YOU WILL DO

- Identify the cable, connector, or interface type and specify the name beside the picture.

■ WHAT YOU WILL NEED

- Pictures of various cables, connectors, and interfaces
- Network+ curriculum book

■ SETTING UP

- Download pictures from the Internet of RJ-45, RJ-11, AUI, coaxial, and BNC t-connectors.
- Download pictures of ST & SC fiber connectors, and terminating resistors used in a 10BASE2 network
- Identify cable type
- Identify connector type
- Identify interface type
- List name beside the picture
- Place the lab in your journal

Token Ring Troubleshooting

■ INTRODUCTION

The Network+ technician should be familiar with how data flows on a token-ring network. The understanding of how data flows on token-ring networks is vital to the design and the troubleshooting process of these types of networks.

The strange logical and physical topology of the token-ring network will be examined.

A typical token ring troubleshooting problem will be presented.

■ WHAT YOU WILL DO

- Map the logical and physical topology
- Troubleshoot data flow on token ring with a fault condition

■ WHAT YOU WILL NEED

- Network+ curriculum book
- Token ring network topology

■ SETTING UP

- Map the logical and physical topology
    Depict in a drawing the logical and physical topology.
- Troubleshoot data flow on a token-ring network with a fault
    Trace the data flow when faults occur in a Token Ring network.
- Place the Lab in your Journal

Part I

Host 2 on MAU A seizes the token and transmits data to Host 3 on MAU B on the network shown. What is the physical path that the data takes to complete each sequence of the transaction?

Part 2

What is the logical topology of the network shown? What is the physical topology of the network shown?

Part 3

Users on the token-ring network depicted below on MAU A or MAU B are unable to reach hosts on MAU C. What is the probable cause?

FIGURE 5.1.1

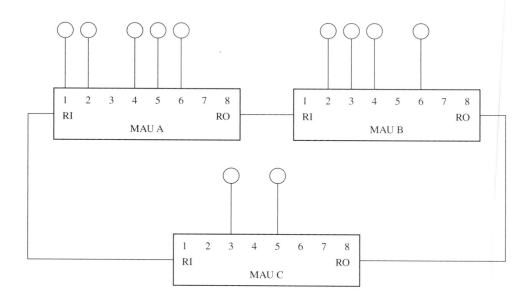

Token Ring
Paths

■ INTRODUCTION

The Network+ technician should be familiar with the components of token-ring networks. The STP cabling, MAU, MSAU, and tokens used to support data transmission on token-ring networks will be examined.

     The knowledge of how data flows on a token-ring network is also supported in this lab.

     The strange logical and physical topology of the token-ring network will be examined.

■ WHAT YOU WILL DO

- Specify data flow on a token-ring network
- Map the logical and physical topology
- Troubleshoot data flow on token ring with a fault condition

■ WHAT YOU WILL NEED

- Network+ curriculum book
- Network topology example

■ SETTING UP

- Trace the data flow on a token-ring network
  Trace the flow of data in the token-ring network provided.
- Map the logical and physical topology
  Depict the logical and physical topology in the drawing.
- Place the lab in your journal

Part 1

Host 2 on MAU A seizes the token and transmits data to Host 3 on MAU C on the network shown. What is the path that the data takes to complete each sequence of the transaction? When is the data transmission complete and the token released into the network for another station to use?

Part 2

What is the logical topology of the network shown? What is the physical topology of the network shown?

FIGURE 5.2.1

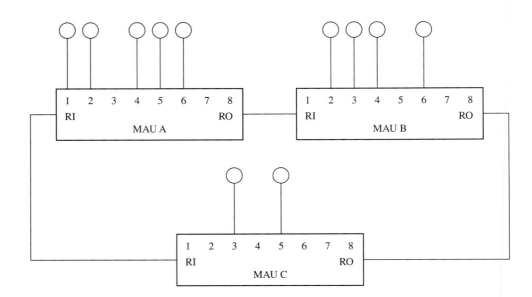

Direct Connection for Two Computers

LAB **6.1**

■ INTRODUCTION

The connection of two computers is the simplest of possible network installations. The connection of two computers without the use of a hub or switch is made possible through the use of a crossover cable. This cable, covered in an earlier lab, crosses the send and receive pairs of the cable [second (orange) and third (green) pairs]. If a hub or switch is used to connect two or more computers, a straight cable is used.

The direct connection of two computers through a single crossover provides only the basic need of file and printer sharing between the two machines. No other device will be able to join the network unless a hub or switch is used.

Both computers must have a NIC installed and properly configured. IP addressing is covered in a later chapter. Both computers must be addressed with an IP address in the same network. Follow the procedures outlined in the NIC installation lab. Use a 10.1.1.1 address on one machine and 10.1.1.2 on the other with a 10.1.1.254 default gateway on both machines. The subnet mask can be set at 255.255.255.0.

The NIC should show a green light when it is properly connected and configured. Most NICs have this feature indicating connection speed.

■ WHAT YOU WILL DO

- Connect two computers
- Test the connection
- Share folders

■ WHAT YOU WILL NEED

- Two computers equipped with NICs
- One crossover cable or two straight cables and a hub

■ SETTING UP

Gather the computers, hubs, and cables needed for this lab.

Part I Connect Two Computers

1. Plug the crossover cable you created in an earlier lab into the NICs on both computers.

2. Right-click *Network Neighborhood* > Choose *Properties* > Highlight *TCP/IP linked to your NIC* > Select *Properties* > Select *Specify an IP address* from the options.

Enter the addressing information provided earlier in this lab. DNS services do not need to be configured for the purposes of this lab.

3. Choose *Start > Settings > Network and Dial-up Connections >* Select *Local Area Connection >* Click *Properties.* A box with your NIC identified should appear (Windows 2000) under *Connect Using.*

4. Click *Install >* From the list (*Select Network Component Type*) choose *Client > Add > Client for Microsoft Networks > OK.* (You may need your Windows 2000 Installation CD.)

5. Files and printers are shared in the manner illustrated in step 4. Click *Install >* From the list select *Service >* Click *Add >* Select *File and Printer Sharing for Microsoft Networks >* Click *OK.* Make sure that a check mark is shown next to File and Printer Sharing.

Part 2 Test the Connection

1. Look at the NIC on each computer for a link light indicating a connection.

2. On each machine, click *Start > Programs > Accessories > Command Prompt.*

3. At the command prompt, type the command **ipconfig/all**. You should see a screen similar to the one shown below.

4. The settings that you applied to the NIC should appear. This is one way to verify your settings are correct.

5. Ping the NIC by typing **ping 127.0.0.1** at the command prompt. You should get a successful response similar to the one shown below.

```
C:\>ping 127.0.0.1

Pinging 127.0.0.1 with 32 bytes of data
Reply from 127.0.0.1:bytes=32time<10ms TTL=32
Reply from 127.0.0.1:bytes=32time<10ms TTL=32
Reply from 127.0.0.1:bytes=32time<10ms TTL=32
Reply from 127.0.0.1:bytes=32time<10ms TTL=32
```

6. Ping your IP address by typing the following: **ping 10.1.1.1** or **ping 10.1.1.2**. A successful response indicates a connection to your own card.

```
C:\>ping 10.1.1.1

Pinging 10.1.1.1 with 32 bytes of data
Reply from 10.1.1.1:bytes=32time<10ms TTL=32
```

```
Reply from 10.1.1.1:bytes=32time<10ms TTL=32
Reply from 10.1.1.1:bytes=32time<10ms TTL=32
Reply from 10.1.1.1:bytes=32time<10ms TTL=32
```

7. Finally, ping the other computer connected to you with the command **ping 10.1.1.2** or **ping 10.1.1.1**. A successful response indicates a connection to the remote computer. Successful output should look as follows:

```
C:\>ping 10.1.1.2
Pinging 10.1.1.2 with 32 bytes of data
Reply from 10.1.1.2: bytes=32time<10ms TTL=32
Reply from 10.1.1.2: bytes=32time<10ms TTL=32
Reply from 10.1.1.2: bytes=32time<10ms TTL=32
Reply from 10.1.1.2: bytes=32time<10ms TTL=32
```

Part 3 Share Folders

1. If the steps above indicate that your configuration and connection are successful, try sharing folders in the following manner. Browse to the folder you want to share > Right-click it > Select *Sharing* > Click the *Sharing* tab > Click the *Share this folder* button > Enter a share name in the *Share Name* text box > Enter a descriptive comment if desired > Specify a user limit under *Maximum Allowed* or *Allow* $\times$ *Number of Users* > Set permissions on the share using share permissions or NTFS permissions.

2. Verify that you can access the files on the remote computer.

3. Place the lab in your journal.

Connecting to a Remote Network with a VPN

LAB **6.2**

■ INTRODUCTION

The ability to share sensitive information over the Internet is made possible through VPN. This lab provides the information necessary to complete this task. VPN (Virtual Private Network) connections are advertised as being easy to establish using Windows 2000 or Windows XP. In this lab you will roll up your sleeves and give it a try.

When a VPN connection is established, an IP address from the remote network is assigned to your computer. The address is taken from the private address pool of the remote network. The data you send is encapsulated inside another IP packet addressed to the remote VPN server using its public address. When the data arrives at the remote VPN server, the original data and addresses are given to the remote network.

The connection is established using a logon name and password verifying a relationship. The data can be encrypted.

The data security possible through the Internet makes VPN a very useful protocol for users who connect to a corporate network through a dial-up, DSL, or cable modem connection.

■ WHAT YOU WILL DO

- Connect to a remote VPN connection
- Send data

■ WHAT YOU WILL NEED

- Local computer running Windows 2000
- Remote computer running Windows 2000
- Hostname or IP address of the remote VPN connection

■ SETTING UP

You can connect through an ISP or through your LAN connection. Just follow the steps.

Part I Set Up the VPN Connection

1. Click *Start*, *Settings*, *Network and Dial-Up Connections*, and open the *Make New Connection* icon.

2. Select *Dial-Up to Private Network through the Internet*, and click *Next*.

3. If you need to use your dial-up connection to access the Internet, you can select that option here. Then click *Next*.

4. If you are using a LAN connection to tunnel, click *Do not dial the initial connection.*

5. The hostname or IP address of the remote dial-in server is entered next. (e.g., vpn.farplaces.com or IP address)

6. Choose whether the connection name and phone number should be available to all users of this computer or to you alone.

7. Choose a name for the connection. You may also place a shortcut on the desktop.

8. Click *Finish*. Windows will try to start the connection immediately, but cancel and right-click the connection icon and select *Properties*.

9. Five tabs are now shown.

10. The General tab presents the hostname or IP address of your VPN connection server and the dial-up connection used, if that is necessary. If you set up the VPN connection over a LAN, uncheck the *Dial Another Connection First* check box.

11. The Options tab defaults should be adequate.

12. The Security tab can verify that the Require Secured Password and Require Data Encryption options are set. Automatically Use My Windows Logon Name and Password can be checked to use your current login name and password on the remote system.

13. The Networking tab defaults should be adequate.

14. The Sharing tab specifies what is to be shared on the connection. Default settings are usually adequate.

Part 2 Dial a VPN Connection

1. Click the connection icon on the desktop that you created earlier.

2. Provide the username and password, if needed, for a dial-up connection.

3. Provide the username and password for access to the remote network. Select *Connect*.

4. The remote VPN server will now be contacted, the username and password verified, your computer registered on the network, and the connection status revealed on the Taskbar.

Part 3 Share Printers, Files, and Folders

1. Use the established connection to share printers, files, and folders.

2. When your tasks are completed, right-click the connection icon and select *Disconnect*.

3. Place the lab in your journal.

Network Utilities/ IPconfig & Ping

■ INTRODUCTION

Several utilities are included with Windows operating systems. The person who is Network+ certified must have the ability to identify the output of these utilities and understand the output for the purposes of troubleshooting a network.

IPconfig is a vital utility available at the MS-DOS command prompt. IP address information from all your network adapters and active connections can be scrutinized. If your network uses DHCP services, Ipconfig is the only way to find out what your IP address is.

We used some of these related utilities in Lab 6.1 to verify the IP address of our computer, including IPconfig and Ping. The details related to Ping, Tracert, Arp, and other utilities will be covered in chapter 8.

The purpose of this lab is to better familiarize you with the IPconfig utility and the process of pinging your NIC to verify that your NIC is properly configured to participate in your network.

■ WHAT YOU WILL DO

- Check your NIC configuration
- Study the output of the command
- Ping your loopback
- Ping your NIC

■ WHAT YOU WILL NEED

- Computer with Windows operating system installed
- NIC installed from Lab 6.1

■ SETTING UP

Part 1 Start the Command Prompt

1. Click *Start*, *Run*, type **command** for Windows 95/98 or **cmd** for NT/2000 in the text box, and click *OK*.

Part 2 Using IPconfig

1. Type **ipconfig** at the MS-DOS prompt and press *Enter*. The IP address, subnet mask, and default gateway will appear.

Part 3 Expanded Output

1. Type **ipconfig?** at the prompt.

2. What are the possible commands that can be appended to the ipconfig command? _____

_____

_____

_____

3. The all option adds the output of the domain name and address information for the DNS server.

4. Try typing **ipconfig /all**.

5. Did you notice the extra output? Note: DNS information and the domain name will appear if these services are active on your network.

6. The definitions of the various fields follow:

A. *Hostname* is the name you or your administrator gave your computer.

B. *Primary DNS suffix* is the Internet domain that your computer is a part of.

C. *Node type* is the method that Windows will use to find other computers on your LAN (should be set to Hybrid on Windows 2000 Server and Broadcast on others).

D. *IP routing enabled* reveals whether Windows will pass packets from one adapter to another or whether this computer is an Internet gateway.

E. *WINS proxy enabled* doesn't apply to Windows 2000 Professional.

F. *DNS suffix search list* is the alternative domain name used if the default doesn't match and you type only part of the host name.

G. *Connection-specific DNS suffix* is the domain name for this connection only. (Think dial-up.)

H. *Description* is the manufacturer of the LAN adapter used or the type of dial-up connection.

I. *Physical address* is the MAC address.

J. *DHCP enabled* set to *Yes* means that the adapter is prepared to receive an IP address automatically; *No* means the address was manually set.

K. *IP address* is the IP address for this adapter.

L. *Subnet mask* relates to the part of the IP address that will determine the addresses included in the local LAN.

M. *Default gateway* is the address that packets to outside networks are sent to.

N. *DNS servers* is the IP address of domain name servers this computer knows about.

Part 4 Ipconfig /release_all and /renew_all Commands

1. If your network configuration information is obtained from a DHCP server, the IP address on your computer is provided from the server automatically when your computer boots. The server has specific configuration information stating how long your "lease" on this IP address will last.

2. The address obtained from the DHCP server can be removed from your computer by typing **ipconfig /release**.

3. In order to get a new IP address without rebooting, type **ipconfig /renew**. Did your computer get the same address it had earlier? ___ Usually this will be the case unless another device booted onto the network and received your previous address from the server.

4. The need for these commands may not be readily apparent to the beginning Network+ candidate. Suffice it to say that there are times when configurations of the network may need to be changed and certain addresses "saved" for certain purposes like print servers. If one of these addresses has already been leased, the need to release and renew comes into play.

Part 5 Ping Your LOOPBACK and NIC

1. The TCP/IP Ping utility by default sends four packets and prints or echoes the result of the four tests.

2. First ping the network software of your computer by typing the command **ping 127.0.0.1**. The ping is sent to the computer you are on and tests the TCP/IP protocol for correct installation and configuration. If this ping fails, remove and reinstall the *Internet Protocol* from *Local Area Connection* in *Network and Dial-Up Connections*. This ping tests the configuration down to the LLC layer of the NIC.

3. Next, ping the IP address of your own computer. At the prompt type **ping A.B.C.D** where A–D is your IP address. If this ping is successful, your configuration is good and everything works theoretically to the jack on your NIC.

4. Now ping the IP address of a computer on your LAN, your default gateway, a known remote host. If this is successful, great. If not, try typing **netstat -s -p icmp** and check the results of your pings.

5. Check your wiring or the NIC of the other computer on your LAN for proper TCP/IP configuration if the connection cannot be made.

6. Place the lab in your journal.

Netstat

■ INTRODUCTION

The Netstat utility will display information about your TCP/IP connections and stats. Computers communicating with you will be displayed in the output of this command. Several different switches can be added to the basic netstat command to filter the results displayed.

The netstat command, when typed at the command prompt, will display all TCP/IP connections that are current between your computer and any others that happen to be serving or receiving services from your computer. The output from the basic form of the command lists the protocol used (usually TCP), the name of the host at each end of the connection, and the port number used at each end of the present connection. It also shows the state of the present connection. This lab will explore the many uses and commands related to netstat.

A TCP connection goes through several stages that can be seen through the use of the Netstat utility. The state of the connection is listed on the far right of the output under the State heading.

■ WHAT YOU WILL DO

- Explore the uses of the Netstat utility
- Match TCP/IP port numbers with the service offered at that port

■ WHAT YOU WILL NEED

- Computer with Windows operating system
- Connection to computer network or to the Internet

■ SETTING UP

Part I The Netstat Utility

1. Click *Start*, *Run*, type **cmd** (or **command** with Windows 95/98), click *OK*, and type **netstat** at the prompt.

2. The output should be similar to the following:

```
Proto    Local Address         Foreign Address          State
TCP      waveguide:4409        www.anysite.com:telnet   ESTABLISHED
TCP      waveguide:3708        anycity.com:80           CLOSE_WAIT
TCP      waveguide:4750        www.anyany.com:80        CLOSE_WAIT
```

3. Notice in the output of the command that the protocol that is used for the session is shown under the heading "Proto". The local host name follows, with the local port number after the colon. The foreign (remote) address (10.0.0.6) or host name (boo.yourcompany.com) follows, with the port number appearing after the colon again. Finally, the state of the session is shown. The various states of a session are:

    A. *Listening:* Your computer has a service it can provide and is waiting for another computer to connect and use it.

    B. *SYN_Sent:* Our computer sent a "dialing" packet out to a remote host but has not received any data back.

    C. *Established:* The computers are connected and can send data in both directions.

    D. *Close_Wait:* Our computer has informed the other that it is ready to end the connection but no response has yet been received.

    E. *Time_Wait:* Connection is closed but still remembered. (Ignore these entries.)

If the netstat command reveals a session in SYN_Sent and will not progress to established, check connectivity with a ping command. If the ping is successful this indicates a problem with the remote server.

4. Several switches can be used with the netstat command to enhance the output. This is a short synopsis of the switches available:

    A. *Netstat -a:* This means that all established connections and services your computer offers to the LAN will be displayed.

    B. *Netstat -n:* Adding this switch keeps the unknown domain name from causing a wait before netstat gives up trying to find it. Only the remote IP address will print if the domain name is unknown.

    C. *Netstat -s* or *-S:* Same output on both. Gives a view of statistics like total packets received, bad packets received, packets too large for the underlying network, packets re-sent due to errors, and so on. Most of this output is not extremely helpful, although seeing whether ping packets are being received by your computer may reveal a connectivity problem.

Part 2 Well-Known Port Numbers

1. Search through the text and on the Internet if necessary to find the well-known port numbers for the following network protocols. This information can be found in RFC 1700. Search the Web for RFC 1700.

Protocol	Port Number	Uses/TCP or UDP
WWW		
SMTP		
FTP		
DNS		
HTTPS		
POP3		
Telnet		
TFTP		
Netbios		
BOOTP		

2. Place the lab in your journal.

NBTSTAT

LAB **7.2**

■ INTRODUCTION

The purpose of this lab is to familiarize you with the utility called NBTSTAT. NBT (Net-Bios over TCP/IP) STAT (Statistics) is a critical tool for problem solving and depends on Microsoft's use of NetBIOS in Windows operating systems. Windows computers are assigned NetBIOS name to allow them to communicate with each other. The idea is that names are easier to remember than IP addresses. Workgroup and domain names are also NetBIOS names. The NetBIOS protocol is not routable, but NetBIOS over TCP/IP is.

Nbtstat displays the name tables for both the local and remote computers and the NetBIOS name cache. If you are using a NIC to access the network, your MAC address will also be included in the output. Nbtstat has a command to refresh the NetBIOS name cache and the names registered with WINS. If the nbtstat command is entered without parameters or switches, it displays the help menu.

■ WHAT YOU WILL DO

- Observe the output of the nbtstat command
- Discover all the possible information revealed with this command
- Discover troubleshooting help available

■ WHAT YOU WILL NEED

- Computer on a network
- Dial-up connection to the Internet

■ SETTING UP

Part I Starting Nbtsttat

1. Click Start, Run, type **cmd** (**command** on a Windows 95/98 machine), and type **nbtstat** at the prompt. The output of this command without switches should look something like what is shown below.

```
NBTSTAT [ [-a RemoteName] [-A IP address] [-c] [-n]
  [-r] [-R] [-RR] [-s] [-S] [interval] ]
-a (adapter status)   Lists the remote machine's name table
                      given its name
-A (Adapter status)   Lists the remote machine's name table
                      given its IP address.
-c (cache)            Lists NBT's cache of remote [machine]
                      names and their IP addresses
```

```
-n (names)              Lists local NetBIOS names.
-r (resolved)           Lists names resolved by broadcast and
                        via WINS
-R (Reload)             Purges and reloads the remote cache
                        name table
-S (Sessions)           Lists sessions table with the
                        destination IP addresses
-s (sessions)           Lists sessions table converting
                        destination IP addresses to computer
                        NETBIOS names.
-RR (ReleaseRefresh)    Sends Name Release packets to WINS and
                        then starts  Refresh
RemoteName              Remote host machine name.
IP address              Dotted decimal representation of the
                        IP address.
interval                Redisplays selected statistics,
                        pausing interval seconds between each
                        display. Press Ctrl + C to stop
                        redisplaying statistics.
```

2. The switches used with the nbtstat command are as follows:
   A. *Nbtstat -a:* Use this when you know the machine name you are looking for.
   B. *Nbtstat -A:* Use this when you know the IP address of the machine you are looking for.
   C. *Nbtstat -c:* This displays the contents of the NetBIOS name cache, the table of NetBIOS names, and their resolved IP addresses.
   D. *Nbtstat -n:* Name table of the local computer. Registered means that the name is registered by broadcast or a WINS server.
   E. *Nbtstat -r:* Displays NetBIOS name resolution stats.
   F. *Nbtstat -R:* Purges the NetBIOS name cache and reloads entries from the LMHosts file.
   G. *Nbtstat -RR:* Releases and refreshes NetBIOS name registered with the WINS server.
   H. *Nbtstat -s:* Displays NetBIOS client and server sessions, attempting to convert the destination IP address to a name.
   I. *Nbtstat -S:* Displays NetBIOS client and server sessions; lists remote computers by the destination IP address only.

3. Headings generated by the nbtstat command are as follows:
   A. *Input:* Bytes received
   B. *Output:* Bytes sent
   C. *Inbound/Outbound:* Whether connection is from this computer (outbound) or from another computer to this one (inbound)
   D. *Local name:* This computer's name
   E. *Remote name:* Connected computer's name
   F. *<03> :* The last byte of a NetBIOS name converted to hex
   G. *Type:* Type of name (unique or group)
   H. *Status:* Indicates whether NetBIOS service is running on remote computer (registered) or whether a duplicate computer name has registered the service and created a conflict
   I. *State:* State of the connections

4. The states of NetBIOS connections revealed by the Nbtstat command are as follows:

   A. *Connected:* Session established
   B. *Associated:* A connection endpoint has been created and linked to an IP address

C. *Listening:* Available for an inbound connection

D. *Idle:* Endpoint open but cannot receive connections

E. *Connecting:* Session in connecting phase and name to IP addressing is being resolved

F. *Accepting:* An inbound session is being accepted and will soon be connected

G. *Reconnecting:* Session trying to reconnect after a failure

H. *Outbound:* TCP connection is being created

I. *Inbound:* Inbound session is in the connection phase

J. *Disconnecting:* Session in disconnecting process

K. *Disconnected:* Local has issued a disconnect and is waiting for confirmation from remote

Part 2 Consider the output

1. Spend some time performing the commands in this lab and observe the output related to the IP address and computer names of the local computer and the remote computers that you are connected to. Consider how this information might be helpful in troubleshooting networks. Make sure you understand how the switches help to refine the output.

2. Place the lab in your journal.

Network
Protocols

■ INTRODUCTION

Protocols are rules relating to how data is exchanged over different networks. Specifications are made as to how data will be organized for transmission over different types of media (copper, fiber, wireless). For many years protocol development lay in the hands of the big corporations that developed proprietary protocols to carry data over their own systems. The Internet with its need for information exchange on a wider scale has changed this. The protocol of choice is now TCP/IP.

A vast number of protocols are nested under the umbrella that is known as TCP/IP. An Internet visit to *www.protocols.com* will reveal just how big that umbrella is. Some of the protocols listed are not familiar to many novice networkers, but there are many valid reasons to explore the many methods of data delivery. An understanding, or at least a knowledge, of protocols and their particular methods will be helpful in diagnosing network problems and securing your network from attack.

■ WHAT YOU WILL DO

- Explore the *www.protocols.com* Web site for information on TCP/IP and UDP protocols.
- Research the various protocols and list the methods they use to pass their important information to others.
- Group the protocols according to performance and method (transport protocols, routing protocols, OSI model layer, function, service, media specifications, authentication, security, network management, etc.)

■ WHAT YOU WILL NEED

- Computer with access to the Internet

■ SETTING UP

Part I Explore **www.protocols.com**

This Web site is full of information about network protocols. Gather whatever information you can acquire about the protocols that are listed on this Web site. Click on the link to view the protocols route map. This represents the OSI model's relationship to protocols in an easy-to-understand way. You can click on a particular TCP/IP or UDP protocol listed in the chart and it will link you to a page entirely about that particular protocol.

Part 2 Research the Various Protocols

Use the protocols route map to search through the protocols and compile information to put in your journal about them.

Part 3 Categorize the Protocols

1. Categorize them in relation to function, layer, media specifications, and so on.
2. Place the lab in your journal.

ARP & RARP

■ INTRODUCTION

The purpose of this lab is to familiarize you with the characteristics of the ARP and RARP utilities. The ARP utility answers the question for the workstation, "What is the MAC address for IP address 192.168.4.2?" The RARP utility answers the question for the diskless workstation, "What is my IP address (I know my MAC address)?"

You can find out what IP addresses are mapped to physical addresses on your network through the use of the arp -a command. It tells us at a glance that our computer has successfully exchanged ARP information with the computers listed in the output. How can this feature be helpful? It may help you determine what layer of the OSI model to check if you encounter network transmission problems. For instance, if our computer has all the IP addresses of each device cached in our ARP table and we are experiencing difficulty communicating with a computer that has an entry in the ARP cache, we could be having a problem with a higher layer protocol.

The RARP entries, revealed by a protocol analyzer as we boot up our diskless workstation, could reveal why our particular terminal did not receive an IP address.

■ WHAT YOU WILL DO

- Download the Ethereal Network Analyzer
- Install Ethereal on a computer
- Get permission to use it on a network
- Observe the ARP and RARP utilities in action

■ WHAT YOU WILL NEED

- Computer
- Internet access
- Permission to use a network analyzer on your network

■ SETTING UP

Part I Download Ethereal Network Analyzer

1. Contact *www.ethereal.com* and follow directions to download a free copy of the Ethereal Network Analyzer.

2. CAUTION: The use of a packet analyzer on a network without expressed written permission could be grounds for dismissal. Network administrators do not like surprises. The safest way to test your skills with an analyzer is on a test network in a lab environment.

Part 2 If Permitted, Install Ethereal on Your Computer

1. Follow the instructions on the Web site.

Part 3 Observe the ARP and RARP Utilities

1. Connect the computer with the Network Analyzer installed onto the network with an address appropriate to the network.

2. ARP entries will time out of the cache after several minutes, so it will be best if the computer you have the Network Analyzer installed on has been disconnected from the network long enough so that when the arp command is issued at the command prompt, no entries are revealed.

3. Start the Network Analyzer and watch the frames tagged as ARP or RARP.

4. Note the source and destination of the frames.

5. Ping several of the computers on your network segment and observe the output. The following is a typical output from a single computer (10.0.1.1) on a network with another computer, which is possibly the address of the default gateway device (10.0.1.2):

```
C:\WINDOWS>arp -a
Interface: 10.0.1.1 on Interface 0x1000002
Internet Address      Physical Address      Type
10.0.1.2              08-00-3e-02-07-8d     dynamic
```

The ARP table may contain several entries indicated as follows:

```
Interface: 192.168.1.112 on Interface 0x2000003

Internet Address      Physical Address      Type
192.168.1.1           00-20-78-c6-78-14     dynamic
192.168.1.101         00-03-47-8f-15-f5     dynamic
192.168.1.102         00-03-47-8f-05-7a     dynamic
192.168.1.103         00-d0-b7-b5-12-24     dynamic
```

Part 4 Add an Entry to the ARP Table Manually

1. Use the command **arp -s** to add a static entry to the ARP table. You could use this command to make sure that an ARP entry never times out of your ARP cache. The syntax for the command is as follows:

```
C:\WINDOWS\arp -s 192.168.1.210 08-00-2B-3C-9E-AA
```

After you enter the arp command, perform it at the prompt and observe the entry in the ARP table.

2. Place the lab in your journal.

IP Addressing Practice

LAB **8.2**

■ INTRODUCTION

The Network+ candidate will be expected to know how to address devices on a network and how to plan for optimum usage of these addresses when planning a network. In order to perform this task, binary-to-decimal conversions must be understood. The best way to make sure that a network device is properly placed on the intended network segment is to return to the bits and examine the subnets in their simplest form.

The ability to quickly convert binary to decimal and decimal to binary is an essential skill to the Network+ candidate. Perform the steps in this lab in order to develop these skills. Note: It is assumed that you already have an understanding of binary math. If this is not the case, I encourage you to get some tutoring help in this area before you attempt this exercise.

■ WHAT YOU WILL DO

- Complete a computer addressing exercise

■ WHAT YOU WILL NEED

- Pencil and an eraser

■ SETTING UP

Part I Create a Reference Sheet

1. Binary is expressed in two numbers, 0 and 1. Create a chart in groups of eight similar to the design below. Each X represents a place holder to help us express our binary-to-decimal chart. Draw this chart on scratch paper and from right to left in the chart put 2's over the first column, 4's over the next, 8's , 16's, 32's, 64's, 128's, and so on. Repeat this pattern over the next group of eight X's until you have numbered the whole chart. This chart should help you begin to see the decimal representation of the addresses in the way the computer sees them. Remember, there are no breaks in the way a computer sees this address. It sees the IP address as a 32-bit number. The representation in decimal is interded only to make it easier for you to represent an IP address and enter it correctly.

XXXXXXXX . XXXXXXXX . XXXXXXXX . XXXXXXXX

Part 2 Complete the Practice Exercises

Fill in the blanks in the following exercises and compare answers with someone else.

Binary to Decimal and Back Again

Express the following numbers in binary form.

Number	Binary Number
245	
13	
143	
165	
255	
244	
246	
189	
175	
1	
14	
12	

Express the following numbers in decimal form.

Number	Decimal Number
10101001	
10101010	
11110000	
01101101	
11111111	
01111111	
00111111	
00011111	
00001111	
01100001	
01111101	
00000111	

IP Addresses

Identify classful IP addresses:

1. First 2 bits of class B address
2. First bit of class A address
3. First 3 bits of class C address
4. First 4 bits of class D address
5. First 4 bits of class E address

For classful IP addressing:

1. Class A addresses use _____ octet(s) for the network portion of the address.
2. Class B addresses use _____ octet(s) for the network portion of the address.
3. Class C addresses use _____ octet(s) for the network portion of the address.

Identify the range of assignable IP addresses for:

1. Class A IP networks
2. Class B IP networks
3. Class C IP networks

Identify the private address range for:

1. Class A IP networks
2. Class B IP networks
3. Class C IP networks

Loopback address space

Loopback address space is anything in the 127.0.0.0–127.255.255.254 range. These addresses are used to test the functionality of the TCP/IP stack. If 127.0.0.1 (the test address most often used) is pinged and a reply is received, the TCP/IP stack is configured properly. Pinging the IP address configured on the NIC verifies that everything is working properly (theoretically) to the NIC port.

In a classful (not subnetted) IP network, in which network are the following addresses located?

1. 195.2.4.3
2. 172.15.3.2
3. 122.2.5.254
4. 95.2.55.245
5. 1.2.3.56

Place the lab in your journal.

Ping and Tracert Utilities

LAB **8.3**

■ INTRODUCTION

Ping and Tracert are two closely related utilities that are used to test connectivity and path selection to local and remote hosts. We will begin our lab with the study of the ping command and then explore the tracert command.

The ping command is a tool often used to test for connectivity between hosts. When you enter the command (ping 10.1.1.1), a few packets of data are sent to the computer address you specified and a reply is received. If the reply is from your own gateway or any other address than the one you specified, it's time to use the tracert command to find where the connection failed. If the ping command works properly and returns a reply from the host you specified, you know that your network wiring, TCP/IP software, and any routers between you and the remote computer you pinged are working properly. Ping can also be used to obtain the IP address of a host for which you know only the name and domain (e.g., ping *www.Anyhost.com*).

Tracert works similarly to the ping command with one exception: It marks the first few packets it sends, preventing them from traveling past more than one router. The router returns them as undeliverable with its own IP address included. Tracert then repeats the process marking the packets so that they can pass only two routers. The next hop router returns the packets as undeliverable with its own IP address included in the message. This process continues until each packet reaches the address you specified initially or it fails. This produces a mapping of the route the packets take to a destination and reveals the point where the packets dropped if the earlier presented ping was unsuccessful. This ability to pinpoint the failure point in a connection makes the tracert command valuable.

Keep in mind that several companies will not accept a ping or tracert packet from any source.

■ WHAT YOU WILL DO

- Use the ping command to verify a local and a remote host
- Use the tracert command to verify the path taken to destinations

■ WHAT YOU WILL NEED

- Computer connected to a network or with an Internet connection

■ SETTING UP

Part I Use the Ping Command

1. Click start, run, type **cmd** (**command** on Windows 98), and type **ping 127.0.0.1**. This is the command to ping the loopback address of your NIC. This address could be any 127.x.x.x address. The 127 network is reserved for loopback testing purposes. The ability to ping the loopback ensures that TCP/IP is installed and functioning.

2. Next, ping the address of your own computer. Type **ping X.X.X.X** where X is the address of your computer. Refer back to the IPconfig lab if you've forgotten how to determine what your IP address is and how to configure it. A response indicating successful completion of the ping indicates that your configuration is good through your NIC.

3. Try pinging another host on your local network if you are on a LAN. If you are connected to another computer at home, try pinging its IP address. These pings should be successful. If not, troubleshoot the connection.

4. Try pinging the hostname of your own computer. Were you successful? Your computer is successful at resolving a hostname to an IP address. Try pinging the hostname of another computer on your network. Were you successful? If the hostname has spaces in it, you will have to put the hostname in quotes to be successful. The command line syntax does not like spaces.

5. Typing the command **ping /?** will show the options for the ping command. The options available with the ping command are as follows:

ping-t	Ping the specified host until stopped. To see statistics and continue...Type Control Break. To stop the output...type Control C.
ping-a	Resolve addresses to hostnames
ping-n count	Number of echo requests to send
ping-l size	Send buffer size
ping-f	Set Don't Fragment bit
ping-i TTL	Time to Live
ping-v TOS	Type of Service
ping-r count	Record route for count hops
ping-s count	Timestamp for count hops
ping-j host-list	Loose source route along host-list
ping-k host-list	Strict source route along host-list
ping-w timeout	Timeout in milliseconds to wait for each reply

Part 2 Tracert Command

1. Type the command **tracert www.anyhost.com**, replacing *anyhost* with a familiar Web site. If the earlier pings were successful, tracert should reveal how the packets arrived at their destination.

2. You can also type **tracert X.X.X.X** with the IP address of a local or a remote host you know about and trace the path the packets take to the destination you chose.

3. An interesting look at the tracert command can be found by doing a search for the Neotrace software download available at many sites online. There is a 30-day trial version you can download and play with. Shown below is the output of a tracert command to a site in Martinique. This Neotrace program is a really great way to view the path of your packets. A time is associated with each hop your data takes, which helps you analyze problematic flows with your data stream.

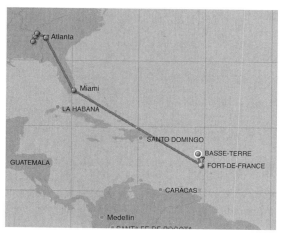

4. Press Control+C in order to stop the tracert output if it can't find a path without waiting for the default 30 attempts.

5. Type **tracert** and press Enter to see the available options with the tracert command. The options are as follows:

tracert-d	Do not resolve addresses to hostnames
tracert-h maximum hops	Maximum number of hops to search for target
tracert-j host-list	Loose source route along host-list
Tracert-w timeout	Wait timeout milliseconds for each reply

6. The -d option will speed up the tracert process because each router's name will not have to be looked up.

7. Place the lab in your journal.

Configuring Novell/NetWare Systems

■ INTRODUCTION

The terms "Novell" and "NetWare" are sometimes used to refer to the same thing; the NetWare line of servers and operating systems. NetWare operating systems started as a system offering file and print services to other workstation operating systems. According to the information given on the NetWare Web site, the installation of a file server requires very little additional work directly to the server after the operating system is installed. The file server is controlled from a client workstation. The result of the installation is that the file access is transparent to the end-user. This means that the file and application access is provided without the end-user knowing whether the files or applications reside on the local computer or on the server.

Logins are made to what Novell calls the Directory Service. The Directory Service is a database that serves as the end-user's link to all the network servers. The network administrator decides what services a user is allowed to access on the network.

The purpose of this lab is to inform you and prepare you to install NetWare servers and clients.

■ WHAT YOU WILL DO

- Plan the network
- Set up the hardware
- Install software
- Administration tasks

■ WHAT YOU WILL NEED

- Computer with Internet access
- Access to a NetWare network (Optional)

■ SETTING UP

Part 1 Planning

1. How many devices will be supported?
2. Gather facts on how many clients each server can support.
   A. Perform Internet research on the Novell Web site.
   B. Search for local users of Novell products.
3. Are connections from client to server needed over WAN links?

4. Will routers be used in the network design?
- A. Routers can be used to provide GNS requests seeking services that reside on distant networks.
- B. Check the router used for support of the IPX/SPX protocols.

Part 2 Hardware Setup

1. The server and the client should be connected together with Ethernet hardware.

2. The location of printers, routers, switches, and other network devices should be considered.

Part 3 Installing Software

1. Ensure LAN or WAN connectivity between the servers and the clients.

2. The installation process uses DOS to boot and install the NetWare operating system.

3. First you select the language you want to use during the install process. The option *Accept the license agreement or quit...* appears.

4. The install process will now look for NetWare partitions. If they do not exist, the install process will help you set them up.

5. Is it a new install or upgrade?

6. Select a file server name. Make it meaningful.

7. Select what type of directory service to use.

8. The recommendation by Novell is to accept the defaults on the additional settings. The install process will detect device drivers, check devices, set regional settings, mount the volumes, and specify the network protocols for each board.

9. Decide whether to use IP or IPX as a routing protocol. IPX addressing is very simple. IP is more complex but offers agreement with the Internet. You can select both.

10. IPX addresses are defined by a network number that consists of 32 bits. The remaining 48 bits of the IPX address are defined by the MAC address of the machine. Simply stated, pick out a network number and IPX will do the rest.

11. IP networks require defining a DNS server. NetWare states this can be ignored on a small network.

12. Select a password for user Admin.

13. Put in your license disk.

14. Select the context for the license and the components to install. Search the Novell Web site for the functionality of each service.
- A. Novell certificate server
- B. LDAP services
- C. NetWare management portal
- D. Storage management services
- E. Novell distributed print services
- F. Novell enterprise Web server
- G. NetWare Web manager
- H. NetWare news server
- I. NetWare FTP server
- J. IBM websphere application server
- K. NetWare Web search
- L. Novell DNS/DHCP server
- M. Novell Internet manager services
- N. WAN traffic manager services
- O. NetWare multimedia server

15. Install client software.
   A. Install the CD-ROM and answer the questions with the file server running.
   B. Reboot the machine after installing, log in as admin, and you're in business.

Part 4 Administrative Tasks

1. NWAdmin is the principal tool used to administer NetWare.

2. Locate the *SYS* volume in the *MY COMPUTER* folder and select *PUBLIC*, *WIN32*, and *NWADMIN32* to run.

3. You'll be able to add printers, users, or anything else a network might need from your new position as administrator.

4. Place the lab in your journal.

Troubleshooting IPX/SPX Networks

LAB **9.2**

■ INTRODUCTION

The Network+ candidate can expect to be exposed to Novell networks. There are many Novell networks installed. Finding problems quickly and getting the network up and running is the job of the Network+ certified technician.

The basic troubleshooting model is molded to fit the methods of the Novell network. Following a systematic plan is the best way to repair any network.

■ WHAT YOU WILL DO

- Examine a troubleshooting model for NetWare networks

■ WHAT YOU WILL NEED

- Computer connected to the Internet
- Access to a NetWare network

■ SETTING UP

Examine a Troubleshooting Model for NetWare Networks

1. Follow the steps indicated in order to solve NetWare problems.
2. Check the following client parameters:
   A. Is the right frame encapsulation used?
   B. Is Client for NetWare installed and the user logged in?
   C. Is the NIC configured correctly?
3. Local router configuration (if used)
   A. Use show commands to verify router configuration
   B. Check state of interfaces
4. Ping out throughout the network. If you find a router that does not respond to IPX pings then:
   A. Check the routing table using the show IPX route command and see if a route to the server is in the routing table
   B. Check network number specs for duplicate addresses
   C. Check to see that IPX routing is enabled and debug to see that SAP and RIP packets are being exchanged
5. Check the server configuration for the following:
   A. Internal and external addresses
   B. Name of the server
   C. Encapsulation matches

71

D. Number of users that are allowed versus the number that are trying to log on
E. CPU overutilized (should be 65% or less)
F. Is enough hard drive space available to operate?
G. Is memory space overutilized?
H. Are service requests being serviced by virtual memory?
I. Do two servers have the same name?
J. Is a protocol bound to the NIC?
K. Are there any unresolved Interrupt or DMA conflicts?
L. Is encapsulation the wrong type?

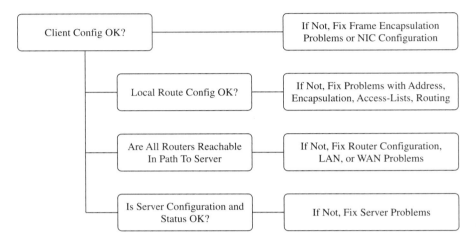

6. Place the lab in your journal.

NetWare Protocols

■ INTRODUCTION

The purpose of this lab is to familiarize the Network+ candidate with the protocols used in Novell/NetWare networks. Familiarity with the protocols and a visual guideline of how the protocols fit into the OSI model will promote understanding relative to network troubleshooting.

The different encapsulation methods used in NetWare networks present a potential problem. A problem common to NetWare networks is having one encapsulation type on a server and another on a client. Devices such as routers or switches that are used to connect NetWare servers and clients should be properly configured with the appropriate encapsulation type.

■ WHAT YOU WILL DO

- Define the various protocols used in NetWare networks
- Place the protocols in the OSI model table
- Define the various NetWare encapsulation methods

■ WHAT YOU WILL NEED

- Access to the Internet
- Resource book related to NetWare protocols and encapsulation methods

■ SETTING UP

Part I Define NetWare Protocols

1. Research the definitions of the following protocols and terms used in NetWare networks.

- A. NOS
- B. SAP
- C. NCP
- D. SPX
- E. IPX
- F. NLSP
- G. RIP
- H. GNS
- I. Ethernet/IEEE 802.3
- J. Token Ring 802.5
- K. Fast Ethernet

    L. FDDI
    M. PPP
    N. HSSI
    O. ISDN
    P. ATM
    Q. NetBIOS
    R. IPX routing updates are sent every _____?
    S. Layer 4 connection-oriented protocol

Part 2 Place NetWare Protocols in OSI Table

1. Place the protocols that are listed in Part 1 in the OSI table next to the corresponding layer of the OSI model.

Layer	Name				
7	Application				
6	Presentation				
5	Session				
4	Transport				
3	Network				
2	Data Link				
1	Physical				

Part 3 Define NetWare Encapsulation Methods

1. Research the following list of NetWare encapsulation types and reflect on the importance of choosing encapsulation methods that are in agreement on clients and servers.

    A. Ethernet_802.3   a.k.a.   novell-ether

    _____

    B. Ethernet_802.2   a.k.a.   sap

    _____

    C. Ethernet_II   a.k.a.   arpa

    _____

    D. Ethernet_SNAP   a.k.a.   snap

    _____

2. Place the lab in your journal.

Switches versus Hubs

LAB **10.1**

■ INTRODUCTION

The ability to recognize the differences between switches and hubs is a necessary skill. An understanding of how traffic is sent by these two devices will assist the Network+ candidate in determining traffic bottlenecks.

If a network is capable of 100 Mbps, would you prefer that each device shared all this bandwidth or that each device had access to the full available bandwidth? The devices on your network that require large amounts of bandwidth can occupy single ports of switches rather than sharing the available bandwidth with every other device. Of course, if cost is the defining factor in your network design, a hub may be the only way to connect your network devices when using UTP media.

■ WHAT YOU WILL DO

- Examine various network topologies
- Determine the number of collision domains
- Determine bandwidth available to each host on the network

■ WHAT YOU WILL NEED

- Network topology maps
- Knowledge of how switches and hubs work

■ SETTING UP

Part 1 Examine Network Topology

1. Observe the differences in the presented networks.
2. Determine traffic flow to gateway device.

Part 2 Determine Number of Collision Domains

1. Count collision domains and check results with instructor.
2. Make sure your assessment is correct based on the devices used.

Part 3 Calculate the Bandwidth Available

1. Determine bandwidth available on each network device.

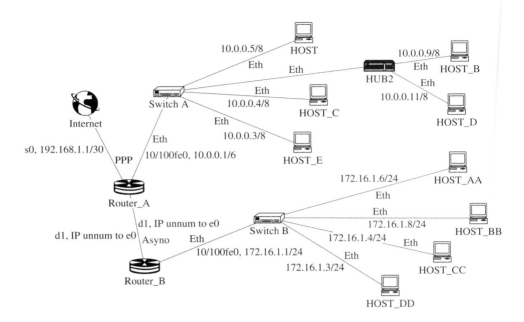

1. What would the default-gateway address configuration be on the hosts connected to the Ethernet interface on Router_A?

2. What would the default-gateway address configuration be on the hosts connected to the Ethernet interface on Router_B?

3. What is the total number of collision domains in the 10.0.0.0 network?

4. What is the total number of collision domains in the 172.16.0.0 network?

5. Is the link between the Internet and Router_A considered to be a collision domain?

6. Each device is equipped with a NIC capable of running at 100 Mbps. How much bandwidth is available to each host listed?

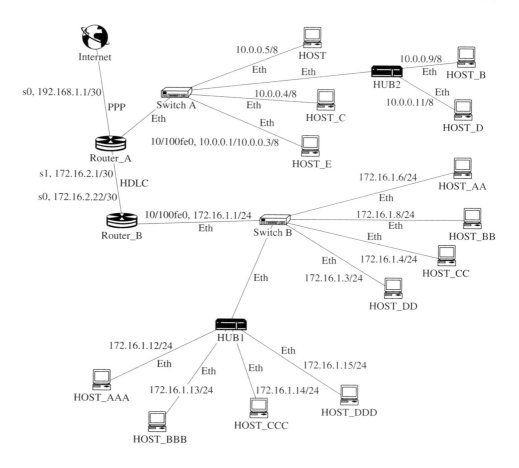

7. What would the default-gateway address configuration be on the hosts connected to the Ethernet interface on Switch B?

8. What would the default-gateway address configuration be on the hosts connected to the Ethernet interface on Hub 1?

9. What would the default-gateway address configuration be on the hosts connected to the Ethernet interface on Hub 2?

10. What would the default-gateway address configuration be on the hosts connected to the Ethernet interface on Switch A?

11. Is the link between Router_A and Router_B considered to be a collision domain?

12. What is the total number of collision domains in the 10.0.0.0 network?

13. What is the total number of collision domains in the 172.16.0.0 network?

14. Is the link between the Internet and Router_A considered to be a collision domain?

15. Each device is equipped with a NIC capable of running at 100 Mbps. How much bandwidth is available to each host listed?

Part 4 Place the Lab in Your Journal

Router Basics

■ INTRODUCTION

The purpose of this lab is to acquaint you with the steps required to accomplish the basic configuration of a router. Each router is configured in a different way. The syntax of the commands required and the interfaces supported by each router platform are of most concern to the Network+ candidate.

The routing protocols supported on router platforms determine either the selection of the router based on the desired protocol or the selection of a viable routing protocol based on the limitations of the router in use.

Routers operate at layer 3 of the OSI model. There is more latency involved in a network path decision that requires the services of a router to arrive at a destination. This just means that the use of an additional device required to pierce another layer of the OSI model adds to the time needed to process the data. Layer 3 switching was referenced in the text, which basically requires the services of the router for an initial packet in a data stream, and all subsequent packets are switched based on the decision made on the initial packet.

The Network+ candidate should learn as many aspects of networking as possible. It is outside the context of this lab to give a full lesson on router configuration. Keep in mind that we are only scratching the surface in the complex world of routing. A router SIM that provides the ability to enter the necessary commands can be purchased, but there is no replacement for actually installing the cables and driving a real router.

■ WHAT YOU WILL DO

- Learn basic steps to router configuration
- Determine addressing scheme for network represented

■ WHAT YOU WILL NEED

- A router or router SIM would be preferred in order to practice router configurations
- In lieu of a router to experiment with, at least follow the commands based on the following network produced with Cisco Configmaker

■ SETTING UP

Part 1 Observe Basic Router Configuration Steps

1. Follow the network diagram and observe the instructions for the configuration of a Cisco 2514 (Router_A) and a Cisco 2501 (Router_B) router. Comments are placed in the configuration to guide you.

Part 2 Observe Proper Addressing Scheme

1. The Network+ trainee will observe that all the addresses depicted on this network are in fact private addresses. Real-world addresses should not be used for practice unless of course you own those addresses. Remember that private addresses such as those we are using are not able to propagate on the Internet. They can be used between you and your ISP or internally by your ISP, but will not work on the Internet. It is a common practice for ISPs to use a private addressing scheme for connecting their T1 customers. The explanation of what a command accomplishes is printed in bold print.

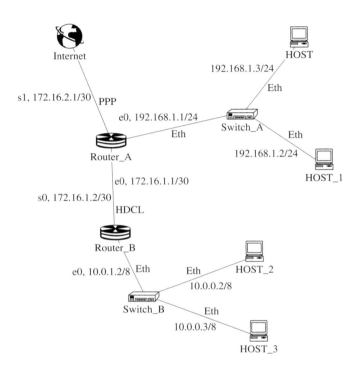

```
!!
**************************************************************
*****
!Router_A.cfg - Cisco router configuration file
!Automatically created by Cisco ConfigMaker v2.6 Build 6
!  Thursday, August 28, 2003, 08:12:49 PM
!
!Hostname: Router_A
!Model: 2514
!
**************************************************************
*****
```

!We will pass over the explanation of the next few commands and
!concentrate on interface and routing protocol configurations.
```
service timestamps debug uptime
service timestamps log uptime
service password-encryption
no service tcp-small-servers
no service udp-small-servers
```

```
!The next command configures a name for the router.
hostname Router_A
```

```
!This configures a password.
enable password aaaa
```

```
!This says this is not a DNS server.
no ip name-server
```

```
!This allows the use of the first subnet in a network.
ip subnet-zero
```

```
!This prevents the router from searching for a host if you
!type a bad command.
no ip domain-lookup
```

```
!This enables ip routing.
ip routing
```

```
!The following 5 lines pertain to configuration of the
!interface. Interfaces are down by default, so the "no shut"
!command turns them on. The description command identifies
!the interface and the ip address command assigns an IP address
!to the interface.
!interface Ethernet 0
no shutdown
description connected to Switch_A
ip address 192.168.1.1 255.255.255.0
keepalive 10
```

```
!The following lines pertain to configuration of the inter
!face that is not used.
interface Ethernet 1
no description
no ip address
shutdown
!
```

```
!The following 5 lines pertain to configuration of the inter
!face, causing it to be up,have a description, an IP address,
!and the encapsulation method on the serial line to Router_B.
interface Serial 0
no shutdown
description connected to Router_B
ip address 172.16.1.1 255.255.255.252
encapsulation hdlc
```

```
!The following 5 lines pertain to configuration of the in
!terface, causing it to be up, have a description, an IP ad
!dress, and the encapsulation method on the serial line to the
!Internet.
interface Serial 1
no shutdown
description connected to Internet
ip address 172.16.2.1 255.255.255.252
encapsulation ppp
!
```

```
!The following line states that RIP will be our routing
!protocol for the listed networks.
router rip
version 2
```

```
network 192.168.1.0
network 172.16.0.0
passive-interface Serial 1
no auto-summary
!
```

!This command permits the use of CIDR addresses.
```
ip classless
!
```

!The ip route statement defines a path out of the network to
!ward the Internet for all packets.
!IP Static Routes.
```
ip route 0.0.0.0 0.0.0.0 Serial 1
no ip http server
snmp-server community public RO
no snmp-server location
no snmp-server contact
!
```

!Configure the passwords for our console connection.
```
line console 0
exec-timeout 0 0
password aaaa
login
!
```

!Configure the passwords for telnet connections to our
router.
```
line vty 0 4
password aaaa
login
!
end
!Router_B.cfg - Cisco router configuration file
!Automatically created by Cisco ConfigMaker v2.6 Build 6
!Thursday, August 28, 2003, 08:13:59 PM
!
!Hostname: Router_B
!Model: 2501
**********************************************************
******
```

!We will pass over the explanation of the next few commands and
!concentrate on interface and routing protocol configurations.
```
service timestamps debug uptime
service timestamps log uptime
service password-encryption
no service tcp-small-servers
no service udp-small-servers
!
```

!The next command configures a name for the router.
```
hostname Router_B
!
```

!This configures a password.
```
enable password aaaa
!
```

!This says this is not a DNS server.
```
no ip name-server
```

```
!
```

!**This allows the use of the first subnet in a network.**
```
ip subnet-zero
```

!**This prevents a lengthy search if we type a bad command.**
```
no ip domain-lookup
```

!**This enables IP routing.**
```
ip routing
!
```

!**The following 5 lines pertain to configuration of the**
!**interface, causing it to be up, have a description, and an**
!**IP address.**
```
interface Ethernet 0
no shutdown
description connected to Switch_B
ip address 10.0.1.2 255.0.0.0
keepalive 10
!
```

!**The following 5 lines pertain to configuration of the**
!**interface, causing it to be up, have a description, an IP**
!**address, and an encapsulation method.**
```
interface Serial 0
no shutdown
description connected to Router_A
ip address 172.16.1.2 255.255.255.252
encapsulation hdlc
!
```

!**This interface is not configured or used here.**
```
interface Serial 1
no description
no ip address
shutdown
!
```

!**The following line states that RIP will be our routing**
!**protocol for the listed networks.**
```
router rip
version 2
network 10.0.0.0
network 172.16.0.0
no auto-summary
!
```

!**This command permits the use of CIDR addresses.**
```
ip classless
```

!**These commands turn off the router's capability to act as an**
!**HTTP server or SNMP server.**
```
no ip http server
snmp-server community public RO
no snmp-server location
no snmp-server contact
!
```

!**Configure the passwords for our console connection.**
```
line console 0
exec-timeout 0 0
password aaaa
```

```
login
!
!Configure the passwords for telnet connections to our router.
line vty 0 4
password aaaa
login
end
```

2. Place the lab in your journal.

Routing Protocols

■ INTRODUCTION

An understanding of routing protocols is an objective of the Network+ exam objectives. The stated focus of Network+, taken from the exam objectives, is primarily on four routed protocols. You learned in the curriculum the difference between routed and routing protocols. The 3.11 Network+ objective specifies the need to know how to select the appropriate NIC and network configuration settings for a network configuration. The focus of this objective is on the host configuration. The routing objective must be explored to fully understand how packets are routed from source to destination.

■ WHAT YOU WILL DO

- Research routing protocol characteristics
- Complete a table based on your research

■ WHAT YOU WILL NEED

- Network+ book
- Internet access for extra research

■ SETTING UP

Part 1 Research Routing Protocol Characteristics

1. Study the list of routing protocols and determine their type (distance-vector, link-state, hybrid), the metric they use to determine the distance to remote networks, convergence characteristics, interior or exterior gateway protocol, update method including time, algorithm used, and supported features such as CIDR, multicasting, and so on.

Part 2 Complete Routing Protocol Information Table

1. Complete the tables with all applicable information. Can you find the administrative distance for each of the routing protocols? If so, put that in the Features column. Write under the Protocol heading whether the protocol is an open standard or proprietary.

Protocol	Type	Metrics	Update Method	Features
RIPv1				
RIPv2				
IGRP				
EIGRP				
OSPF				
BGP				
IS-IS				
NLSP				

IGPs	Convergence Characteristics	EGPs	Convergence Characteristics

Distance-Vector Protocols	Link-State Protocols

2. Place the lab in your journal.

PGP (Pretty Good Privacy)

LAB ▮ ▮**.**▮

■ INTRODUCTION

The study of network security would not be complete without exploring the various methods of encryption. PGP (Pretty Good Privacy) was produced by Phil Zimmerman. You can read all about the development, features, and procedures for using PGP on this Web site: *http://web.mit.edu/network/pgp.html*.

PGP features the use of the best cryptographic algorithms and includes public-key encryption and certificates of authority. It provides an unlimited distribution of source code and documentation and is not controlled by any government or standards organization. The best thing about it is that is freeware.

After you install PGP, you will have to generate a key pair. One key will be a public key and the other will be a private key. Plug-ins are available on the Web site for the e-mail software that you use. Publish the public key that you generate on the PGP server available on the Web site. Practice sending encrypted messages to your friends. Of course, they will have to generate a public key for you to download and use. They can download your public key from the server so that they can encrypt messages and send them to you.

Several links are listed on the Web site that lead to documents relating to frequently asked questions. There are also links to purchase books written by Phil Zimmerman and others relating to PGP.

■ WHAT YOU WILL DO

- Access this Web address: *http://web.mit.edu/network/pgp.html*
- Download PGP
- Follow directions related to generating keys and sending files

■ WHAT YOU WILL NEED

- Internet access
- Compatible operating system

■ SETTING UP

Part I Access PGP Web Site

1. *http://web.mit.edu/network/pgp.html* is the Web address.

Part 2 Download PGP

1. Follow the directions to download the file that corresponds with your platform (operating system).

Part 3 Generate Keys

1. Follow the listed directions to generate public and private keys.

2. Publish your public key to the PGP server.

3. Have a friend or classmate do the same.

Part 4 Send an Encrypted E-Mail

1. Send an encrypted e-mail using your friend's public key.

2. Receive and decrypt an e-mail using your private key that was encrypted and sent by your friend.

3. Place the lab in your journal.

Software Firewall

■ INTRODUCTION

The following lab will assist the Network+ candidate in the process of installing a software firewall. There are many software firewall products available today. The one we will be talking about, ZoneAlarm, is freeware. It can be found at the following Web site: *http://www.zonelabs.com/store/content/home.jsp*

Zonelabs offers many variations of their software firewalls on this Web site. Only one is listed as free. The features of the free version are somewhat limited, but it is functional. You may want to purchase the product after you see how effective the free version is.

Users with an "always-on" connection to the Internet like DSL or cable modem are encouraged to install some kind of firewall protection on their machines. You can access the Gibson Research Corporation Web site for a computer checkup at *www.grc.com*. They offer many free tools to check your computer for vulnerablilties.

■ WHAT YOU WILL DO

- Access the Zonelabs Web site at *http://www.zonelabs.com/store/content/home.jsp*
- Download the free version of ZoneAlarm
- Practice using the software firewall and note any problems

■ WHAT YOU WILL NEED

- Personal computer
- Internet access

■ SETTING UP

Part I Access the Zonelabs Web Site

1. *http://www.zonelabs.com/store/content/home.jsp*

Part 2 Download the Freeware Version of ZoneAlarm

1. Choose the software and download it.
2. Install it on your computer.

Part 3 Practice Using the Software

1. Access the Internet and observe the output of the software.

2. List below any unusual things you observe about the information that the software produces and any difficulties in using the program.

_____

_____

_____

3. Place the lab in your journal.

Virus Protection

LAB **11.3**

■ INTRODUCTION

The purpose of this lab is to expose the Network+ candidate to the threats posed to networks through the use of various forms of malicious code.

Virus attacks can be mounted from outside or inside a network. They can be characterized as accidental harm to a network or be the result of a planned attack. They can be generated by the novice using scripts and attack strategies downloaded from Black Hat sites or may be the work of highly motivated attackers armed with organized attack strategies and a large amount of CPU power.

It doesn't really matter whether the person who takes down your network is a professional or novice. What matters is whether or not you are prepared for a disaster and whether your response is adequate. The only way perhaps to fully secure your network is to disconnect it and turn all the computers off, but even then someone could steal your hard drive. Every effort should be made to secure your data as much as is possible, weighing the importance versus the cost of that security implementation.

Virus-scanning programs are a vital part of any plan to secure your network from the damage caused by malicious code. A daily upgrade of virus definitions is a good practice. It takes only one successful attack to convince you of the importance of adequate virus protection.

Some of the more popular virus scanners are McAfee, Norton, InoculateIT, Kaspersky, F-Secure, AntiVirus eXpert, Panda, and Norman. A search for virus scanners on your favorite search engine will lead you to some objective surveys relating to the various iterations of virus scanners.

■ WHAT YOU WILL DO

- Define the categories of security threats
- Examine several virus-scanning software versions
- Install the virus-scanning software of your choice

■ WHAT YOU WILL NEED

- Textbook
- Internet access for virus-scanning software research
- Purchase of virus-scanning software

■ SETTING UP

Part I Define These Security Threats

1. Virus
2. Boot sector virus

   3. File virus

   4. Macro virus

   5. Multipartite virus

   6. Trojan horse

   7. Worm

Part 2 Search For Virus-Scanning Software

   1. Perform an Internet search for virus scanners and purchase the one you choose.

Part 3 Install Virus-Scanning Software

   1. Install the software based on the manufacturer's instructions.

   2. Make sure you have the latest virus definitions and operating system fixes installed, even if you have a virus scanner.

   3. Place the lab in your journal.

E-Mail Client Configuration

LAB 12.1

■ INTRODUCTION

There are several different versions of e-mail client software. Research the various e-mail client software versions on the Internet. Talk to your friends and colleagues about the e-mail client software that they prefer in order to decide which one you will use.

For the purposes of this lab, we will install Netscape Mail and configure the software as our default method for sending and receiving e-mail. We'll explore several facets of the software and discover how to send and receive mail using Netscape Mail software.

Most ISPs provide some form of e-mail handling software as part of their basic package. The ISP's e-mail server is accessed with a Web browser, which acts like e-mail client software and allows the user to send and receive e-mail messages with or without the use of proprietary e-mail software loaded on the user's computer.

Practice attaching files to e-mails and determine how difficult it would be for some unauthorized person to access the attachment and manipulate the file in some way. This is meant to demonstrate the necessity for the encryption and key sharing practices demonstrated in the labs in chapter 11.

■ WHAT YOU WILL DO

- Install Netscape Mail software
- Configure the e-mail client using the wizard
- Send e-mails to a friend and verify receipt
- Ask for reply e-mails to verify configuration

■ WHAT YOU WILL NEED

- Netscape Mail software or similar software
- Internet access

■ SETTING UP

Part 1 Install Netscape Mail Software

1. Follow installation instructions.

Part 2 Configure E-Mail Client

1. Open Netscape Mail.

2. Follow the instructions presented by the wizard to set up a new account. Choose *Email account* and click *Next*.

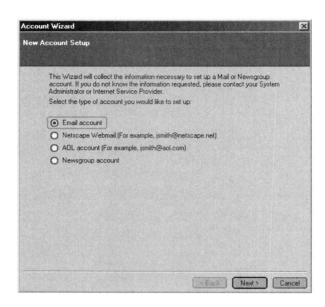

3. Enter your name in the first box, and the address others will use to send e-mail to you in the second box. This second entry will be determined by the ISP you use. The entry included is for our friend from the book, Joe Tekk. He is using an ISP or domain called stny.rr.com to receive his e-mail. For your setup, include your own name and the domain or ISP you will use to receive your e-mail.

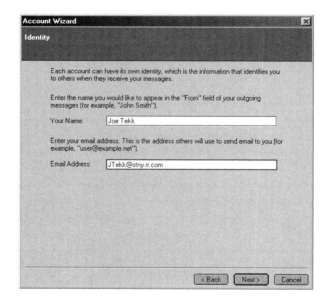

4. Choose the type of server that will be used to receive your e-mail. This type of information will typically be provided by your network administrator or ISP. The information entered will be similar to that shown in the following example.

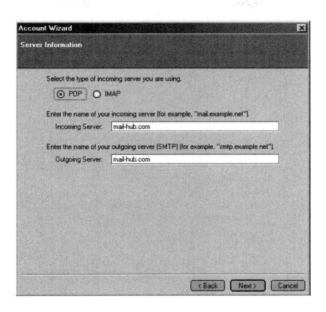

5. Enter the name you will use to receive e-mail. You and your ISP will participate in finding a unique e-mail address. Most of this information will be entered dynamically when you load the software provided by your ISP and fill in the blanks for the wizard.

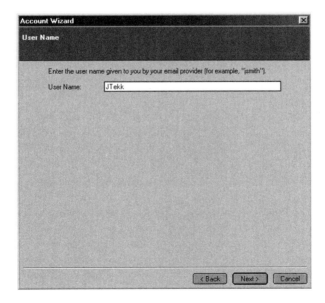

6. Enter the way you would like to reference this e-mail account. It will help distinguish it from other e-mail accounts that you use.

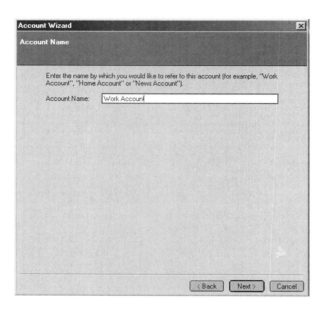

7. The following screen dump shows the information that you have just configured. Click *Finish* to indicate that the information listed is correct or go back if changes are to be configured.

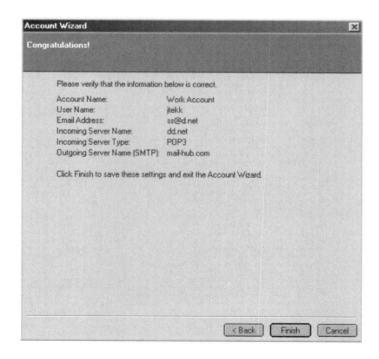

8. The following is the default Mail & Newsgroups page. From this page we can choose to view the mail located on your e-mail server or download e-mail to a folder.

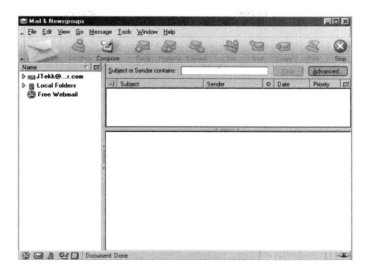

9. After the configurations are finished, you will see a page similar to the one shown below. Choose whether or not to use Netscape 7.0 as your default mail application.

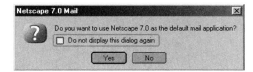

10. Select *Compose* to see the following page and write an e-mail. Enter the address of the person you wish to write to, compose the message, and send it.

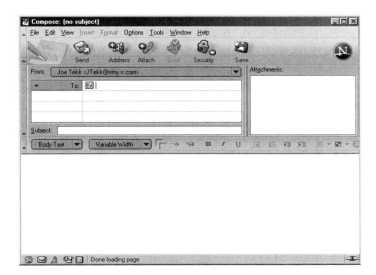

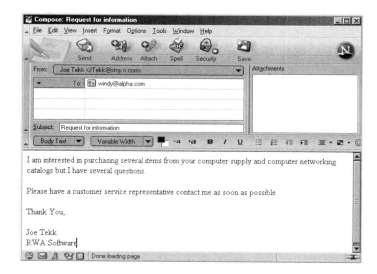

11. You can use the Security tab to reveal whether or not your e-mail messages are encrypted. Remember the PGP encryption software in your efforts to secure your e-mail messages.

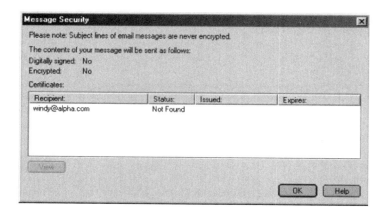

12. The following screen represents what you will see if you access your personal address book in your e-mail software.

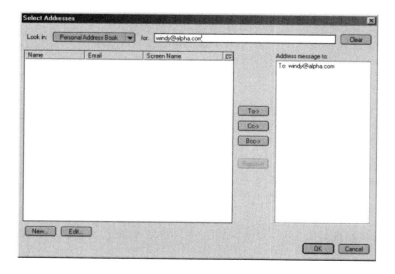

13. When you click *Send* on the message composition page, a popup will appear informing you that your message is being sent.

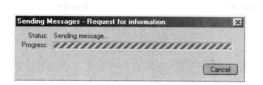

14. If for some reason the message cannot be sent, an error box will appear informing you that your e-mail was not sent.

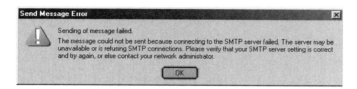

15. If you need help determining how to perform a task related to sending or receiving e-mail, click on the *Help and Support* page.

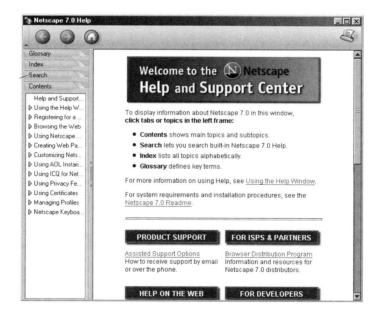

Part 3 Send E-Mails to a Friend

1. Practice composing an e-mail.

2. Try attaching various file types to an e-mail. Click on *Attach* to start the process and follow directions.

3. Notice the attached file in the box indicating attachments.

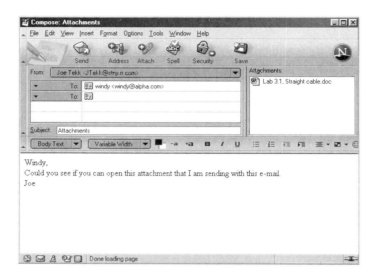

Part 4 Receive and Read E-Mails from a Friend

1. Receive and read received e-mails.
2. Open attachments received with e-mails.
3. Place the lab in your journal.

Zipping E-Mail Attachments

■ INTRODUCTION

The process of sending e-mails with files attached can be a difficult if not impossible process if the intended attachments are too large. Some e-mail servers limit the size of received attachments to 1 MB. The attachment size should be limited to 1 MB. If the file that you need to send is larger than that, try sending several e-mails with parts of the file attached.

Another method of attaching a file is to zip the file before you attempt to send it. After the zipping process is done, check the file to make sure that it meets the size restrictions that are normally imposed.

WinZip is a popular choice for performing this task. This lab will attempt to instruct you in the basics of zipping and unzipping files. WinZip offers the Classic format or the Wizard format. Both methods have their pros and cons. Experiment with both methods and find the one that you prefer. The Wizard method should prove to be the easiest for the beginning zipper, but finding your file after you zip it can be a problem for some of us. Remember to select a location that meets your needs. Switching between the two methods is easy, as you will see in the following steps.

■ WHAT YOU WILL DO

- Select and zip a file
- Compare the size of the files before and after zipping
- Attach a zipped file to an e-mail
- Unzip a file

■ WHAT YOU WILL NEED

- WinZip software
- Computer with Internet access
- Configured e-mail client software

■ SETTING UP

Part I Select and Zip a File

1. Choose a 1 MB or greater sized file from your computer

2. Open WinZip. The Classic version is shown below.

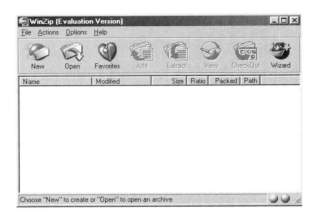

3. Click on the *Wizard* button. A wizard start box will be displayed as shown.

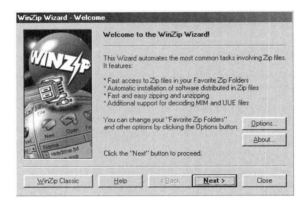

4. Read the information in the box and proceed by clicking *Next*. The following activity box will be displayed, prompting you to either unzip an existing Zip file, update an existing Zip file, or create a new Zip file. Our present process is to zip a document. Choose *Create a new Zip file*.

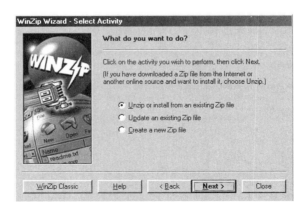

5. The following box should appear. We'll create a file called testzip. Notice that the file will be located in the *C:\My Documents* folder, just in case you want to find it later. Click *Next*.

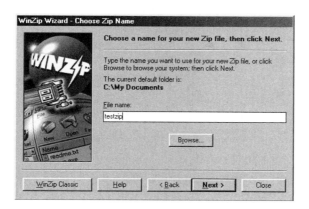

6. From this window you can choose to add files or folders to your *testzip.zip* folder, or you can drag and drop files or folders from *Windows Explorer*.

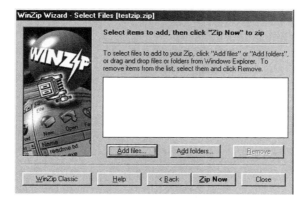

7. Shown is the output from either method. I selected *Add files...* and chose the file to zip.

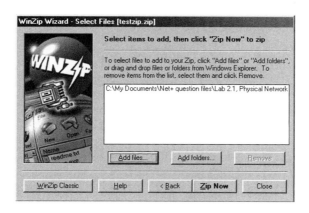

8. Choose *Zip Now* in order to zip the files that we have included.

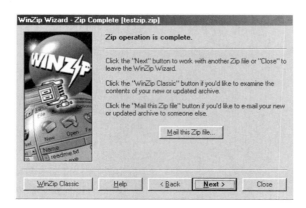

9. The zipping is done. Choose *Close*. Now notice that the Zip file we created called *testzip* is found in *My Documents*.

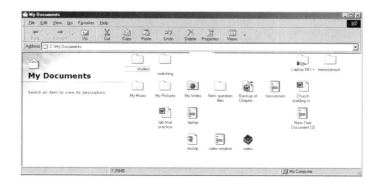

Part 2 Compare File Size Before and After Zipping

1. Check the properties of the file before zipping and after to determine how much the size of the file is reduced by zipping.

Part 3 Attach a Zipped File to an E-mail

1. Now return to Lab 12.1 and compose an e-mail from those directions.

2. Click *Attach*.

3. Choose our *testzip* file that we created and send the e-mail with our Zip file attached.

Part 4 Unzip a Zipped File

1. Select the *testzip* file we created in the *My Documents* folder.

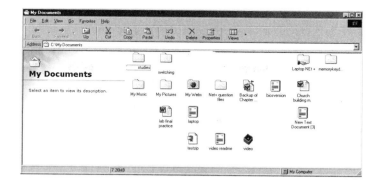

2. When you click on the *testzip* file, the following WinZip window will open.

3. Click *Next*.

4. Choose *Unzip or install* from "testzip.zip".

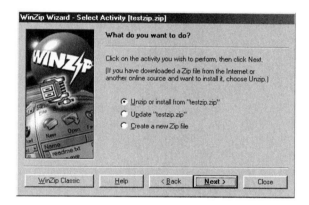

5. Click *Unzip now*.

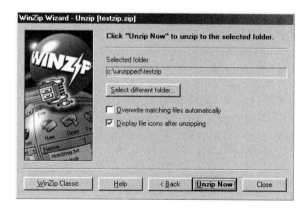

6. The file will unzip and the files that we placed in the *testzip* folder will appear.

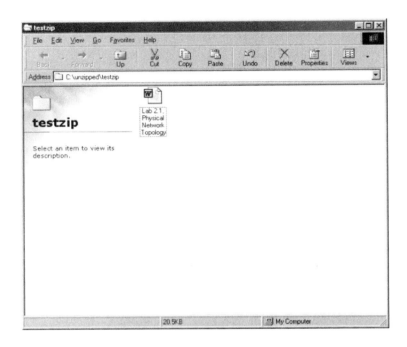

7. Now that you have used the Wizard approach to zipping, go back and try to navigate through the Classic approach.

8. Place the lab in your journal.

E-Mail Analysis

■ INTRODUCTION

E-mail analysis is made possible through the use of a packet capturing tool. The amount of traffic required to generate a simple e-mail message is amazing to see.

The realization that all traffic, including e-mails, can be captured and decoded should encourage each of us to protect the data we send. The lab on PGP in the previous chapter should help prepare us to send and receive information with confidentiality.

Pay attention to the various protocols used in the process of sending and receiving an e-mail. Note the layers of the OSI model used by these protocols. Some trial version packet sniffers do not permit traffic that is generated by other computers to be analyzed. Practice generating several e-mails and get a friend to send you some and see how much can be gleaned from these tools.

■ WHAT YOU WILL DO

- Download a packet sniffer/protocol analyzer
- Install the packet sniffer on your computer
- Send and receive e-mails during packet analysis
- Document the results

■ WHAT YOU WILL NEED

- Packet sniffer/protocol analyzer
- Permission to use packet sniffer

■ SETTING UP

Part I Download a Packet Sniffer

1. Ethereal is freeware and can be downloaded at *www.ethereal.com.*
2. Instructions for download can be found in the documentation for the software.

Part 2 Install Software

1. Follow installation instructions.

Part 3 Start Packet Analysis

1. Start the packet sniffer.
2. Compose a small e-mail.

3. Send the e-mail.

4. Observe the e-mail packet flow.

5. Decode the packets and read the e-mail.

Part 4 Document Your Findings

1. Copy and paste the results of your packet analysis into Notepad.

2. Place the lab in your journal.

FTP Commands

■ INTRODUCTION

The purpose of this lab is to familiarize you with the various commands available when using FTP to send or receive a file. The primary function of FTP is defined as transferring files efficiently and reliably among host computers and allowing the convenient use of remote file storage capabilities. Even though the commands for FTP are provided in the text, there is value in writing the commands and describing what they do. The more times that you perform a task, the more you solidify the skills needed to succeed.

Remember that FTP is the File Transfer Protocol that uses TCP as its underlying transfer protocol. TCP provides the guaranteed reliability factor for FTP. The operation of FTP is defined in RFC 959.

■ WHAT YOU WILL DO

- Evaluate FTP commands
- Complete command chart

■ WHAT YOU WILL NEED

- Network+ book

■ SETTING UP

Part I Evaluate FTP Commands

1. Study the FTP commands.
2. Find the commands that perform similar tasks.

Part 2 Complete Command Chart

1. Reference the Network+ book for the FTP commands.

FTP Commands

FTP Command	What the command does
!	
Delete	
Literal	
Prompt	

Send	
?	
Debug	
Ls	
Put	
Status (or stat)	
Append	
Dir	
mdelete	
pwd	
trace	
ascii	
disconnect	
mdir	
quit	
type	
bell	
get	
mget	
quote	
user	
binary	
glob	
mkdir	
recv	
verbose	
bye	
hash	
mls	
remotehelp	
cd	
help	
mput	
rename	
close	
lcd	
open	
rmdir	

2. Place the lab in your journal.

FTP Explorer

■ INTRODUCTION

The book refers to Windows-based FTP client programs. FTP Explorer is one of those types of programs. It can be found on the *ftpx.com* web site and is available for free download. For those of you that are more comfortable with a Windows-based program, this method of FTP is for you.

We will go through the steps to install FTP Explorer on your computer and practice accessing files located on remote servers.

■ WHAT YOU WILL DO

- Install FTP Explorer

■ WHAT YOU WILL NEED

- Internet access
- Personal computer

■ SETTING UP

Install FTP Explorer

1. Access the www.ftpx.com Web site.

2. Choose to download with HTTP since most of us are more familiar with a Web page. A box similar to that shown below will appear asking what you want to do. Choose to *Save* this file to disk.

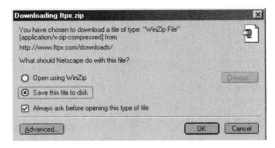

3. A box will appear asking where you want to save the downloaded file and what you wish to name it.

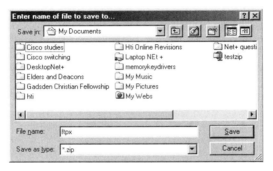

4. When the file is downloaded, a message box should appear with the following message.

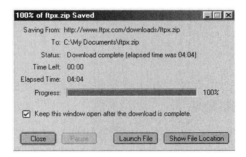

5. Launch the file and WinZip will open to unzip the file. After WinZip finishes unzipping the file, it will ask if you want to *Install now*. Click *Install Now* to install the FTP Explorer program.

6. A message box will appear as follows. Click *Next*.

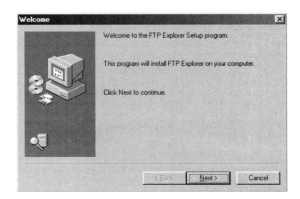

7. The location of the directory that FTP Explorer will install is specified. Click *Next* to accept the default.

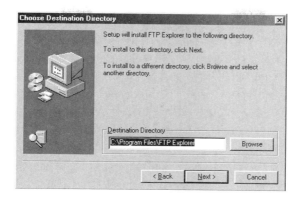

8. You will create a default folder for the program to reside in and then choose what you want the setup program to do from the following list. Read the information and select what you want to accomplish with a check mark. Click *Finish*.

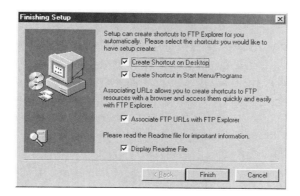

9. The computer must be rebooted before the installation is complete.

10. Place the lab in your journal.

FTP File Transfer Using FTP Explorer

■ INTRODUCTION

In this lab we will use the Windows-based FTP Explorer program that we downloaded and installed in Lab 13.2 to transfer FTP files. We will use the FTP Explorer for the first time and practice transferring files from FTP servers to our personal computer (client).

■ WHAT YOU WILL DO

- Open and set up FTP Explorer
- Transfer FTP files from FTP server to our personal computer

■ WHAT YOU WILL NEED

- Internet access
- FTP Explorer installed

■ SETTING UP

Starting FTP Explorer

1. Click on the *FTP Explorer* icon.

2. The program will open and ask for a valid e-mail address. This e-mail address is necessary for many anonymous FTP logons. Enter your e-mail address in the box provided.

3. FTP Explorer will question you relating to FTP profiles. Click *Yes* and the following box will open.

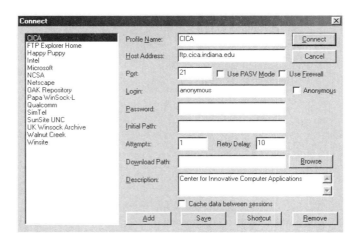

4. The box on the left indicates the various preconfigured profiles. Choose the *FTP Explorer Home* profile and click *Connect*. The following box should appear.

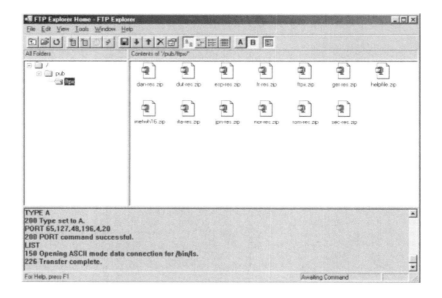

5. Choose the *helpfile.zip* file from the files shown in the right-hand box. A message box will appear specifying where you want to save the file. Specify where you want to save it and click *Save*. A box will appear with the information that the file is being transferred.

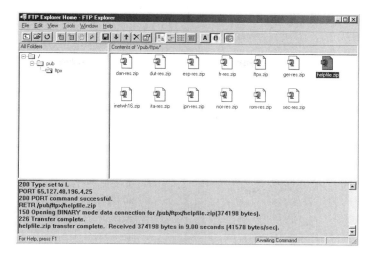

Notice at the bottom of the screen that the *helpfile.zip* transfer was completed and that 374,198 bytes were received in 9 seconds. How easy is that? There are many facets to this program that we will not explore at this time, but feel free to poke around and discover all the possibilities of FTP Explorer.

6. Open the *helpfile.zip* file that we transferred. If you've forgotten how to do that, go back a few labs and find the WinZip lab. The file shown below is the one that we obtained via FTP and is now available for viewing on our computer.

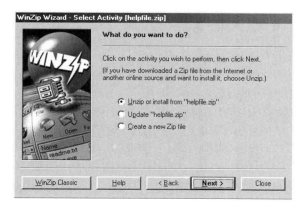

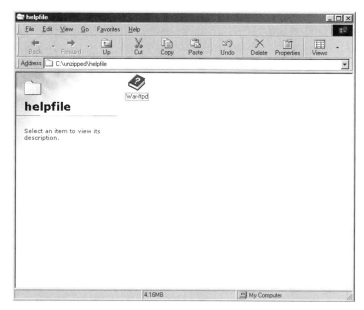

7. Open the file we downloaded. The result should be as shown below.

8. Now you have the ability to obtain files from a remote FTP server and transfer them reliably to your personal computer.

9. Place the lab in your journal.

Image Files

LAB **14.1**

■ INTRODUCTION

This lab will illustrate whether the human eye has the ability to discern the difference in an image saved in various formats. One file format we will use is GIF, which saves the image using lossless compression. We'll also save the same image using the JPEG format, which uses lossy compression methods.

There are many file formats encountered while using the Internet. GIF and JPEG are two of the formats used for still images, and MPEG, MOV, and AVI are commonly used formats for video images.

■ WHAT YOU WILL DO

- Open an image file on your computer that has been saved as a JPEG file. You could also download a picture off the Internet and save it as a JPEG file.
- Save the same image to another folder in a GIF format
- Compare the pictures
- Compare the properties of the two pictures

■ WHAT YOU WILL NEED

- Personal computer with imaging software or at least a paint program

■ SETTING UP

Part 1

1. Open up a picture file on your computer that has been saved using the JPEG format. Notice that the size of the file in the example is 73 KB.

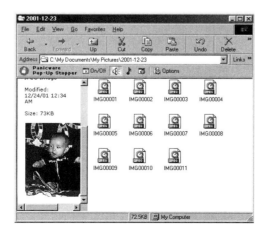

2. Right-click on the file and determine all the information about the file relating to file size, image type, and so on.

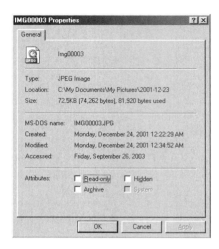

3. Open the file and increase the size of the photo to double size. Observe how the picture tends to lose quality as its size is increased. Reduce the picture to normal size and observe how the grain in the photo image is improved.

4. Save the same image as a GIF file by opening the file and saving it in another folder as a GIF file.

5. Right-click on the file and determine all the information about the file relating to file size, image type, and so on. Notice that the same image saved as a GIF image is now a 58 KB file, smaller than the 73 KB file size when saved as a JPEG image.

6. Can you determine any difference in the clarity of the picture in the double-size format? Reduce the picture to normal size and see if any difference can be seen. The difference in clarity is evident in both size images.

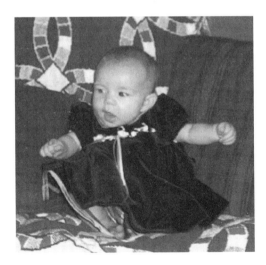

7. The Microsoft Picture It! software saves an image in the MIX format. The images in the examples were saved originally in a JPEG format using Quicktime software.

Part 2 File Format Options

1. *.BMP*: Windows bitmap used in Microsoft Paint and often for desktop backgrounds.

2. *.FPX*: Kodak FlashPIX is a newer imaging application found in high-quality CD-ROM and is similar to the Picture IT! .MIX format.

3. *.JPG*: JPEG is a common, compressed file format used most often for photos. Its image size is relatively small, and it is useful for sending in e-mails or posting on Web sites.

4. *.PNG*: Portable Network Graphics is supported by some newer image applications and works with photos, clip art, and e-mail.

5. *.TIF*: Tagged Image File Format is supported by most image applications and used for clip art CD-ROM.

6. *.GIF*: Graphics Inter-Change Format is used for clip art and solid images rather than photos due to the grain issues with photos.

7. Place the lab in your journal.

Sound File Comparison

LAB **14.2**

■ INTRODUCTION

There are many methods or file formats that can be used to play an audio file. The application software that you are using will probably determine what type of file format you normally use. Windows Media Player, Quicktime, and numerous other software applications support many different types of audio formats. For the purposes of this lab, we will use Sound Recorder to manipulate the way a .wav file is stored and played back. We will then record our observations of how the file sounded after it was changed.

There are two concerns relative to how a sound file is formatted on a PC. The first relates to how a sound is represented to our ears when it is reproduced through the speakers or headphones. The second relates to the amount of space or file size required to store a file in a certain way. There is a direct relationship between file size and sound quality. A larger file generally equates to a better sound image represented at playback.

■ WHAT YOU WILL DO

- Change the way that a .wav file is played back on your computer
- Examine the differences in sound quality

■ WHAT YOU WILL NEED

- Computer equipped with .wav file playback capability

■ SETTING UP

1. Compare a short sound clip saved in different file formats. Click *Start > Programs > Accessories > Entertainment > Sound Recorder*.

2. Click *File > Open*. Select a file to practice on. The file should be long enough to hear and see the effect of different file formats. The file we chose is about a 7-second clip.

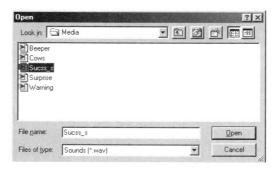

3. We chose *Sucss_s* as our file. Right-click on the file that you choose and note the following properties.

      File name _____

      File size _____

      File type _____

      File extension _____

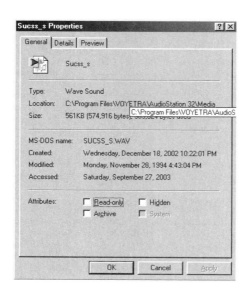

4. Now observe that the file that we have chosen for an example is named *Sucss_s*. It is a .wav sound file. It is 561 KB in size. It is saved as a .wav file.

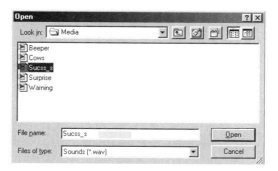

5. Double-click the file that you have chosen. For the purposes of our demonstration we'll click on *Sucss_s*. Play the file.

6. In the *Sucss_s* (*or file of your choosing*)- *Sound Recorder* box, click *File > Save As*. The following box will appear. Notice that the format listed in our example is PCM 22,050 Hz, 16 Bit, Stereo. Choose Change.

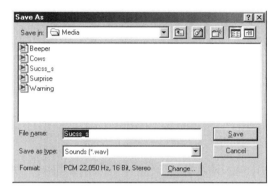

7. Make changes to the format used to play the file. We'll save it as *Sucss_stry*, and then open it with *Sound Recorder* and play it back. Do you notice any difference in the way the sound file is represented? When we played it back using the format shown below, there was evidence of a lot of noise and broken spaces in the sound represented. Did you get a similar response? What are the properties of the file now?

        File name _____
        File size _____
        File type _____
        File extension _____

It is evident that we can change the way that a sound is represented by changing the method in which it is represented for playback. Notice that the file that we changed is now only 70.2 KB is size.

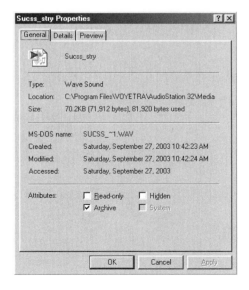

We can see from our lab that the method in which a file is represented affects the quality and size of the file.

8. Place the lab in your journal.

Multimedia File Formats

LAB 14.3

■ INTRODUCTION

The purpose of this lab is to explore the various ways in which multimedia files can be stored and played back on a personal computer. Many media players are available to the end-user. Some are packaged with the music files that you purchase and will "insist" on being loaded before the music is played. The Windows Media Player is the player that we will be using in this lab. Most proprietary media players have their own special group of file extensions used to store multimedia files. Most players will "volunteer" to change all your audio and video file types to those supported by that particular proprietary player.

■ WHAT YOU WILL DO

- Explore the capabilities of your multimedia player
- Explore the difference between downloading and streaming

■ WHAT YOU WILL NEED

- Windows Media Player or equivalent installed on your personal computer
- Internet access

■ SETTING UP

Part 1 File Types

1. Windows Media Player supports the following file types (formats).

File type	File extension
Music CD Playback (CD audio)	.cda
Audio Interchange File Format (AIFF)	.aif, .aifc, and .aiff
Windows Media audio and video files	.asf, .asx, .wax, .wm, .wma, .wmd, .wmp, .wmv, .wmx, .wpl, and .wvx
Windows audio and video files	.avi and .wav
Windows Media Player skins	.wmz
Moving Picture Experts Group (MPEG)	.mpeg, .mpg, .m1v, .mp2, .mpa, .mpe, .mp2v*, and .mpv2
Musical Instrument Digital Interface (MIDI)	.mid, .midi, and .rmi
AU (UNIX)	.au and .snd
MP3	.mp3 and .m3u
DVD video	.vob
Macromedia Flash	.swf

2. RealNetworks players produce file extensions such as .RA, .RAM, .RM, and .RMM.

3. QuickTime uses file extensions such as .QT, .AIF, .AIFC, and .MOV.

4. The RealNetworks and QuickTime file types are not listed specifically, but Windows Media Player will probably convert the files to something that it supports.

5. It can be confusing when you have multiple players on your computer and each player wants to be the default player. Decisions, decisions! Some media players ask you if you want to associate all your multimedia file types with their file system. Others don't. If you're the type who experiments with various media players, you will probably have to associate your files with the player that you choose.

6. The Windows Media Player can be used to organize digital multimedia files on your computer and the Internet.

7. Use the player to access different file types on your computer, compare the results, and record the results below.

Part 2 Full Download Vs. Streaming

1. Try playing an audio file that is stored on your PC.

2. Now access a streaming audio file on the Internet and observe the difference.

3. Try the above exercise with a video file as well.

4. The use of a high-speed Internet connection should provide you, the user, with streaming video and audio with no noticeable difference. Slower Internet connections may not produce the same results.

5. If the file cannot be streamed fast enough to keep the buffers full, the file may produce less than satisfactory results.

6. Place the lab in your journal.

Building a Web Page

■ INTRODUCTION

The purpose of this lab is to familiarize you with the language used to build a simple Web page. This language is called HTML or HyperText Markup Language.

HTML can be described as different sets of instructions that instruct a Web browser on how to represent information to the user. The instructions are HTML tags, which are written in the source code for a particular Web page. The source code looks like a plain text file when viewed except that it contains the HTML tags that control the page.

HTML consists of containers < > and the HTML commands placed inside the containers. The commands inside the containers are used to create the two parts of an HTML tag. The first part (<title>) turns the command on and the second part (</title>) turns it off.

■ WHAT YOU WILL DO

- Build a simple Web page
- Display the Web page
- View the source code you created

■ WHAT YOU WILL NEED

- Computer
- Notepad or similar text editing tool

■ SETTING UP

Part 1 Build a Simple Web Page

1. Open *Notepad*. Click *Start > Programs > Accessories > Notepad*
2. In Notepad make sure that *Word Wrap* is checked as shown

3. Every Web page should include these basic HTML elements if it is to work properly.

> <html>
> <head>
> <title>...</title>
> </head>
> <body>

> What is written here will be displayed on the Web browser.

> </body>
> </head>

4. When you type the command **<html>**, HTML is turned on. In your Notepad document type **<html>**. Press Enter to start on a new line.

5. Next type the command **<head>**. The head section is where you display the title of your Web page. Press Enter.

6. Type **<title>** and add the title **This is My Web Page** next to the command and then close the title like this:

> <title> This is My Web Page </title>

Press Enter.

7. Now close the head section of the page with the command **</head>**. Press Enter.

8. Now open the section of the Web page where all our visible information will be displayed by typing **<body>**. Press Enter.

9. The content of our Web page should be expressed here. Our content will be expressed by typing **The building of a web page is not as difficult as I imagined**. Press Enter.

10. Now close the body tag by typing **</body>**. Press Enter.

11. Close the HTML tag by typing **</html>**. Press Enter.

12. Now save the page with an extension of .html or .htm. Either one can be used, but we will use .html for the purposes of this lab.

13. Click *File*, Save As.

14. Click the arrow on the *Save in* drop-down box and choose the floppy drive.

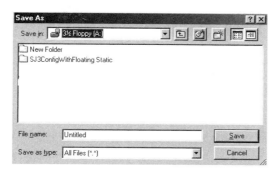

15. After the *Save in* field is set to the floppy drive, type **index.html** in the *File name* portion of the box.

16. In the *Save as type* field, choose the *All Files (*.*)* option.

17. Click *Save*. Your Web page is complete.

Part 2 Display the Web Page You Created

1. Open a Web browser. We'll use Internet Explorer.

2. With Windows Explorer choose *File > Open*. Then click *Browse*.

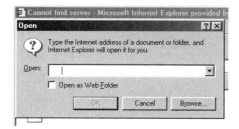

3. Navigate to the floppy drive.

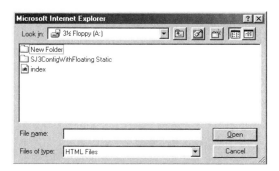

4. Click on the index icon in the window and click *OK* when the *Open* box reappears.

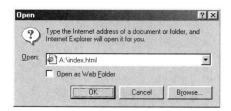

5. Your Web page should appear as follows.

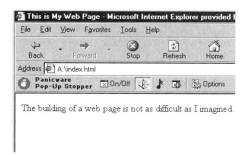

6. Wasn't that easy?

Part 3 View the Source Code

1. The source code of a Web page can be viewed in Internet Explorer by clicking on *View* and then *Source* as shown below.

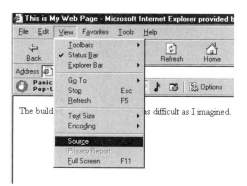

2. On the Web page that you created earlier, click *View* and then click *Source*. It should produce a result like the file you created and saved earlier.

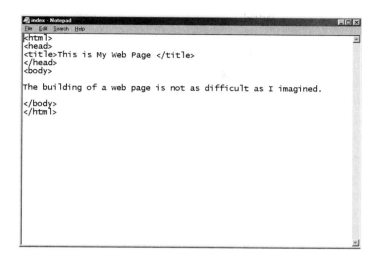

3. Place the lab in your journal.

Writing a JavaScript Application

■ INTRODUCTION

JavaScript is a scripting language that is used to create an active Web page. Web pages can contain areas defined by JavaScript that cause an area of a Web page to open a new window, play sounds, open new URLs, perform math calculations, and numerous other tasks. The result is an interactive Web page.

This lab will introduce some of the rules for using JavaScript. JavaScript is an interpreted language instead of a compiled one. The computer in use has to evaluate the program each time you run it.

The complete knowledge base related to JavaScript is outside the parameters of this book or, for that matter, the Network+ objectives. The need to know about JavaScript lies in the fact that the Network+ candidate should have a working knowledge of the content of Web pages. The Netscape corporation developed JavaScript and a great Web site that maintains many examples and documents related to JavaScript. The JavaScript authoring guide is available online at *http://devedge.netscape.com/library/manuals/2000/javascript/ 1.5/guide/*.

■ WHAT YOU WILL DO

- Explore JavaScript authoring guide
- Write a JavaScript application

■ WHAT YOU WILL NEED

- Computer
- Basic Web page from Lab 15.1
- Text editor

■ SETTING UP

Part I Explore the JavaScript Authoring Guide

1. Visit the Web site. *http://devedge.netscape.com/library/manuals/2000/javascript/ 1.5/guide/* and explore the possibilities of the JavaScript language.

2. Determine a task that JavaScript can accomplish in a Web page.

Part 2 Write a JavaScript Application

1. Open the Web page from the Lab 15.1. Add the following code to the existing Web page code, save the following script as a java.html Web page example, and observe the results.

2. Our existing Web page will undergo several changes.

3. First, we will define JavaScript as our script language right under the head tag opening.

```
<html>
<head>
<script language="JavaScript">
```

4. Insert the code **<!--** to cause web browsers that do not support JavaScript to disregard the text until they find a matching **- ->** .

```
<html>
<head>
<script language="JavaScript">
<!--Hide this script from incompatible web browsers!
```

5. The following lines contain the code that results in the desired function:

```
function pressed () {
alert("I said Don't Press Me");
}
```

6. The braces { } group statements into blocks; a block can be the body of a function or a section of code that gets executed as part of a conditional test.

7. The following closes the script for those Web browsers that do not support JavaScript.

```
<!-- -->
```

8. Next, close the script line like this:

```
</script>
```

9. Now include the code to open up the title:

```
<title> This is my web page </title>
```

and close the title.

10. Close the head with the following command:

```
</head>
```

11. Define the color of the body of the Web page with following the command:

```
<body bgcolor=#bbffff>
```

12. Write the code to create a form with the following commands:

```
<form name="form1">
<input type="button" name="button1" value="Don't
Press Me!" onclick="pressed()">
```

Close the form with the following command:

```
</form>
```

13. Finally, include the text to go on our Web page.

```
The building of a web page is not as difficult as I
imagined.
```

14. Now close the body and close html with the following commands:

```
</body>
</html>
```

15. Now save your document on your floppy disk or anywhere else you wish. Remember to save it as *something.html.*

16. Using your Web browser, open the page you have created and see if it works. When you click on the "Don't Press Me!" button another message should pop up on the browser like this:

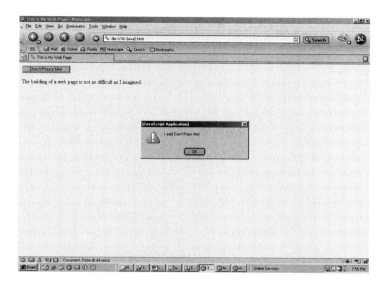

17. The finished code should look like this:

```
<html>
<head>

<script language="JavaScript">
<!--Hide this script from incompatible Web browsers!
function pressed() {
alert("I said Don't Press Me!");
}
<!-- -->
</script>

<title>This is My Web Page </title>

</head>
<body bgcolor=#bbffff>
<form name="form1">
<input type="button" name="button1" value="Don't
Press Me!" onclick="pressed()">
</form>
The building of a web page is not as difficult as I
imagined.
</body>
</html>
```

18. Go to the JavaScript site we referred to in the first part of the lab and explore the many things that can be accomplished with JavaScript.

19. Place the lab in your journal.

Apache Web Server

LAB 15.3

■ INTRODUCTION

The Apache Software Foundation, located at *http://www.apache.org/*, provides the links and methods used to download Apache and set it up. Apache 2.0.47 is listed as the best version of Apache available at this writing. Apache is listed as the Web server used most often. The Web site states that a very high percentage of Web services are now provided by Apache.

■ WHAT YOU WILL DO

- Download and install Apache HTTP server
- Follow Apache ReadMe files to set up Web server

■ WHAT YOU WILL NEED

- Computer capable of running Apache

■ SETTING UP

1. Browse to the Apache Web site *http://www.apache.org/*.

2. Click on the HTTP server link and observe all the instructions related to downloading the HTTP server.

3. Download the file related to your operating system and save as shown below.

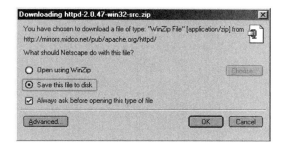

4. Unzip the file and install the HTTP server.

5. Follow instructions from the Apache site related to setup.

6. After installation, explore the services that Apache can provide.

7. Place the lab in your journal.

Network Printing

■ INTRODUCTION

The focus of this lab is to install a printer locally and share it on a network. Can you think of any advantages to having the ability to print on a remote printer? Have you thought of the possibility of printing on a printer that may be across campus or even across town? You could basically send a document to someone by printing over a network.

Anyone can understand the reasoning behind installing a printer to use on a local machine. The type of printer available and the ability of that printer to do a specific job is a valid reason for having more than one printer installed.

If more than one printer is installed, one has to be selected as the default printer. This just means that the printer selected is the one that is always listed in the Print box unless you manually select a different one. You may even have the same printer set up in multiple configurations to allow a printer switch (actually a configuration switch) before a specific print job.

You could add multiple printers in this way (virtually speaking) and still have only one printer. Windows 2000 will create an icon each time you create another configuration. You could name one printer "letters" if you print a lot of text documents. You could name another printer "calendar" if you require a print setup that prints in a landscape mode. The possibilities are endless.

Windows 2000 and Windows XP come with over 3500 printer drivers ready to install. If your printer is not one of the printers covered by this lengthy list of drivers, the printer manufacturer has the driver files, which are normally shipped with a new printer. If the printer is not new and the driver is lost, visit the Web site of the printer manufacturer and find the driver to match your printer.

Installing a printer is often as easy as powering down the computer, hooking up the cables, restarting everything, and clicking *Next* at the wizard prompts. Some of the more selective print setups are not as easy as that. Let's get started.

■ WHAT YOU WILL DO

- Install a local printer
- Install a network printer

■ WHAT YOU WILL NEED

- Computer with administrative access rights
- Additional printer, or connection to another shared printer

■ SETTING UP

Part 1 Install a Local Printer

1. Connect a printer to the appropriate port based on whether it uses a parallel port, a USB port, infrared, or Firewire.

A. Parallel connections are best made with the power off, so shut down the computer and install the cable. Open the Printers folder, double-click *Add Printer* to start the wizard, click *Next*, click *Local Printer*, and turn on *Automatically Detect my Printer*. Click *Next* at the *Found New Hardware Wizard*. Follow the instructions to finish the installation. The printer icon will be added to your Printers folder.

B. USB or Firewire just hot plugs into the computer and is discovered when connected. Follow the directions given by the installation wizard. The printer icon will be added to your *Printers* folder.

C. Infrared must be within the range of your computer's infrared eye. It might install automatically, but if it does not open the *Printers* folder, double-click *Add Printer* (which starts the *Add Printer Wizard*), click *Next*, choose *Local Printer*, and check *Automatically Detect my Printer*. Click *Next* at the *Found New Hardware Wizard* and follow the screen instructions to finish the installation. The printer icon is added to your *Printers* folder.

2. Did Windows on other machines find the remote printer automatically?

3. Can you see it in the Network Neighborhood?

4. If not, specify where the printer is physically connected, what you want to name it, etc.

Part 2 Install a Network Printer

1. Open the *Printers* folder.

2. The *Printers* folder opens and lists the installed printers, if there are any, and the *Add Printer* icon. Double-click the *Add Printer* icon to start the *Add Printer* wizard.

3. *Click Next*. The question "Network or Local?" is asked by the computer. Choose *Network* and click *Next*.

4. Tell the wizard where the printer is and either browse for the path or enter the path manually. For a printer shared over the Web, enter the URL.

5. If you can't quite get the path name down, just leave the name field blank, click *Next*, and browse the list of printers on the network.

6. Highlight the printer you wish to connect to either by double-clicking the *Entire Network* icon or the + sign beside the computer icon in order to display the printers attached to it. Highlight the printer you want to connect to and click *Next*. A connection can also be made by dragging the printer icon from the print server's *Printers* folder and dropping it into your *Printers* folder. Right-click the icon and click *Connect*.

7. If it is necessary to specify the path to the network printer use the syntax: *printserver_name**share_name*

8. A printer shared over the Web should be entered as: *http://www.company.com/corp-printer*

9. Answer any additional questions the wizard asks. Supply drivers if needed.

10. Check and see that the network printer is listed in your *Printers* folder.

11. Print a document.

12. Place the lab in your journal.

Mapping a Network Drive LAB 16.2

■ INTRODUCTION

In the first chapter of the text, it was stated that a computer network is a collection of computers and devices connected so that they can share information. Such networks are called local area networks or LANs. How do we begin to share information in such a way that these files and folders appear as if they were on our local computer? The answer is mapping a network drive.

Have you ever had a file that you needed on one computer while you were working on another computer? This is a regular occurrence if you're constantly changing from your laptop to your desktop computer. Mapping a network drive is a simple process that makes the transfer of files from one machine to another easier. The mapped drive will appear as any of your computer's real physical drives under My Computer. Access to these files will be faster using a mapped drive. The goal of this lab is to teach you how to safely share files and folders, map a network drive, and disconnect a network drive.

Administrators and members of the Administrators and Power Users group can manage file and printer sharing in Windows 2000. File sharing and sharing of other resources on large networks are controlled by network managers. Network managers have the rights to set up shared folders between users on the same machine or users over the network. You must have the same privilege level (administrator or power user) on the computers that you use to perform this lab. Some networks are so tightly controlled that the average user cannot even access a DOS prompt. The idea behind this control is to protect the integrity of data.

■ WHAT YOU WILL DO

- Share a folder
- Map a network drive
- Access the file
- Disconnect the network drive

■ WHAT YOU WILL NEED

- Two computers
- Network connection

■ SETTING UP

Part I Share a Folder

1. Open *Windows Explorer*.
2. Select a folder.

3. Right-click the folder and choose *Properties*. Click the *Sharing* tab.

4. Select *Share This Folder*. Windows will then fill the share name field with the folder name. The folder name should not contain spaces, otherwise it may not be available to Windows for Workgroups users. In this case the folder name could be shortened or abbreviated. A comment can also be inserted to describe the contents of the shared folder.

5. The number of outside users can be limited by setting a user limit.

6. Consider the level of file security that you wish to place on the folder. Other users can be prevented from seeing the shared folder if you add a dollar sign ($) to the end of the share name like this: myfolder$.

Part 2 Map a Network Drive

1. Open *Windows Explorer*.

2. Select *Tools*, *Map Network Drive*.

3. Another optional way to get there is to right-click *My Network Places* and select *Map Network Drive*.

4. Now select an unused drive letter from the drop-down box. Pick a drive letter that has some meaning relative to the file. For instance, if the folder you are mapping to is about Social Engineering, choose drive S.

5. Select the name of the shared folder that the drive letter should be assigned to. The easiest way is to click *Browse* and select the folder from the list. That way the file path will be entered correctly. Find the shared folder and click *OK*. Active Directory networks have an icon called *Directory* where shared resources are grouped in a tree fashion. You will have to pick through the tree and find the computer you're looking for and the shared folder.

6. Now you have two options. If you want the mapping that you have done to reappear each time you log on, check the *Reconnect at login* check box. If you only want to use the mapping temporarily, don't check this box. The mapping will disappear when you log off.

7. If your own Windows username and password does not give you permission to use the shared folder or your username is not recognized at the other computer, select *Connect Using a Different User Name*. Enter the username and password required to access the remote files and click *OK*.

8. Explore *My Computer*. Does the drive letter that you mapped appear? If so, you have successfully mapped a drive. If the mapped drive is not used for a 20-minute period, the mapped drive will turn gray, indicating that the network connection has been terminated. When the drive is used again, it will reconnect and turn black. If the remote computer goes offline, a red diagonal line appears through the drive.

Part 3 Access the Shared File

1. Find the mapped drive that we created.

2. You can double-click on the drive to reveal its contents or right-click and choose from the options there.

3. That's all there is to it.

Part 4 Disconnect the Network Drive

1. Open *Windows Explorer*.

2. Select *Tools*, *Disconnect Network Drive*.

3. Another way to get there is to right-click *My Network Places* and select *Disconnect Network Drive*.

4. A box will appear giving you the option to select any of the mapped drives for disconnection. Click *OK*.

5. If files are currently being accessed by another computer, the reply message will be something like the one shown below. Close the files and save changes before disconnecting.

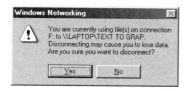

6. You have now safely disconnected your network drive.

7. Place the lab in your journal.

Dial-Up Networking

■ INTRODUCTION

Dial-up networking allows you to connect by modem to a remote network and access files, printers, and other network devices as if you were wired to the LAN directly. Offline folders let you view and use shared network folders and files you select as important even when you're not connected. Windows will keep copies of your network files on your hard drive and keep them up to date. Offline Web pages allow you to mark a Web page and view it even when you're disconnected from the Internet. Virtual Private Networking enables you to have a secure connection through a WAN or over the Internet.

Windows 2000 and Windows XP have the ability to connect to a remote network through the use of a modem and respond as if the computer were directly connected to the local LAN. If the remote network that you are connecting to is using Windows 2000 Server, the receiving connection is handled through Remote Access Services on that operating system. Windows 2000 Professional also can provide some level of Remote Access Services. Let's get on to the connection.

■ WHAT YOU WILL DO

- Create a dial-up connection
- Connect to a remote network
- Disconnect from remote network

■ WHAT YOU WILL NEED

- Computer with Windows 2000 or XP operating system
- Remote network to dial and permission to dial-up

■ SETTING UP

Part I Create a Dial-Up Connection

1. You need to have an installed modem.

2. You need the phone number of the receiving modem for the remote connection, including the area code.

3. The modem that you are using must be compatible with the one used by the remote network. The modem protocols that are supported must be checked. (Is it a V.90, etc.?)

4. The network protocols that the remote network uses (TCP/IP, IPX, etc.) must be enabled on your local computer.

5. The remote network administrator must inform you whether or not DHCP services provide an IP address when you dial in. You may also have to set the IP address of the WINS server.

6. If you want to use e-mail services, the IP addresses of these services might have to be manually configured.

7. You must have the proper username and password to present to the Remote Access Server. These are the same as the regular username and password you normally use when you access the remote network locally. (Remember, we're talking about something like accessing your work network from home or on a business trip.)

8. Now that we know all the little things that we need to make a connection, let's proceed with the creation process.

9. Choose *Settings, Network and Dial-Up Connections*, and open the *Make New Connection* icon.

10. Choose *Dial-Up to Private Network* and click Next.

11. The telephone number of the remote dial-up server is entered, including the area code. Check the *Use Dialing Rules* box to allow Windows to use the right prefix, area code, and the telephone number based on the location you are dialing from. Click *Next*.

12. Windows will now be nice and ask you whether this connection name and phone number is for just you or for everybody. Select all users if all other users on this computer want to connect to the same remote network or if this dial-up connection is used to connect to a remote domain using your roaming profile on that domain.

13. Choose a name for your connection. This name will show up as the name of the connection icon in the *Network and Dial-Up Connections*. You can also choose to put a shortcut to this connection on your desktop.

14. Choose *Finish*. Windows will try to start the connection immediately, but choose *Cancel*, right-click the *New Connection* icon, then select *Properties*.

15. Most of the *Properties* of the connection will remain in their default condition, but some need to be changed.

16. On the *General* tab of the *Properties* box, choose the modem you want to use for this connection if more than one is installed. Set the telephone numbers and dialing rules if necessary.
  - A. *Connect using*: Select the modem
  - B. *Area Code, Phone Number, and Region*: You can specify an alternate telephone number if the company you are connecting to has several access numbers or points.
  - C. *Show Icon in Taskbar*: Gives a connection icon in the task tray when connected.

17. On the *Options* tab:
  - A. *Prompt for Name and Password*: If this box is checked, Windows will always prompt for your remote connection username and password. If left unchecked, Windows will not prompt after the first successful connection but will use the password it remembers.
  - B. *Include Windows Logon Domain*: Check if you're dialing a Windows 2000 domain network and your computer is not a member of the domain you are dialing into.
  - C. *Prompt for Phone Number*: Check this box to display the phone number that Windows is about to dial
  - D. *Redialing Options*: Increase the number of attempts if the remote server you are dialing often gives you a busy signal, and lower the delay from a minute to several seconds to redial quicker.
  - E. *Idle Time Before Hanging Up*: Set this to a reasonable time for the connection to stay up if there is no activity.
  - F. *Redial If Line Is Dropped*: If this box is checked, Windows will redial immediately.

18. On the Security tab:
    A. *Security Options*: Select *Typical* and *Require Secured Password for Windows 2000 and Windows NT RAS*. If the Windows domain name, username, and password are the same as the ones used to sign on to your computer, check *Automatically Use My Windows Logon*.
    B. *Advanced (Custom Settings)*: Check if you are accessing a Shiva RAS. Click *Settings* and select the applicable protocols and the security method used with this connection.

19. On the *Networking* tab:
    A. Choose the network protocols and services enabled for the dial-up connection. It is recommended that you check everything and set TCP/IP properties if needed.
    B. Check *File and Printer Sharing* if you want remote users to have access to your files and printer.
    C. The RAS should take care of the IP, DNS, and DHCP settings.
    D. If the network administrator specifies an IP address for you to set, select *TCP/IP*, then *Properties*, and enter the IP address, mask, and DNS address.

20. On the *Sharing* tab:
    A. Do you want to allow this connection to service your entire LAN? Generally speaking, you will not normally use this dial-up connection to service an entire LAN.

21. If you're using an ISP with different access numbers in different cities that you connect from, you'll have to change these properties as you roam. One option is to set up a separate Network and Dial-Up Connections icon for each access number and use the connection that is applicable to the location.

Part 2 Connect to a Remote Network

1. If you've changed locations involving different area codes or phone systems since your last connection, check your location settings before a dialing attempt.
    A. Open *Control Panel* and choose *Phone* and *Modem Options*.
    B. Select your current location from the list of dial location configurations.
    C. Click *OK*.

2. Choose a profile (if your network provides roaming profiles). Choose one of the following two options:
    A. Connect while you're logged on to your computer and files, printers, and all network resources on the remote network can be accessed. The My Documents folder and desktop will not change, and you will appear to be on your local computer. You can connect without a profile. Make the connection directly without logging out. Use the profile you are presently using on your local (laptop) computer.
        i. Open the connection from *Network and Dial-Up Connections* or through the shortcut you created.
        ii. Enter the login name, password, and domain if they are different from what is on your (local to you/laptop) computer. Adjust the connection number and dialing properties if necessary.
        iii. Click *Dial*. The Progress box is shown dialing, verifying username and password, and registering computer on the remote network.
        iv. If the connection fails, an error box will appear with an explanation.
        v. If the connection is successful, a connection icon will appear in the Taskbar revealing the connection speed.

B. Log off from Windows and then log on with the *Log On Using Dial-Up Connection* option. You will be connected using your user profile on the remote system. Settings for *My Documents*, home directory, desktop, and other preferences will copy to your laptop (local) computer, giving the appearance you're at the office. In order for you to use a remote network with the user profile for that network, log in as follows:

    i. Log off the current Windows connection.

    ii. Click *Start*, *Shut Down*, and *Log off*. Press Ctrl + Alt + Del to show the logon dialog box.

    iii. Choose *Options*, then check *Log On Using Dial-Up Connection*, then *OK*.

    iv. Choose a connection to the network from the drop-down list and click *Dial*.

    v. Enter the username, password, and login domain for the remote network when the *Connect Dialog* box pops up. Select *Dial*.

    vi. Windows will dial, and after the profile settings have been copied, you're on the remote network.

3. Callbacks are required on some dial-up networking connections. A callback is a security feature to ensure that the person calling the network is who they claim to be. The network administrator will arrange for the phone number used to call your computer back.

A. Choose *Network and Dial-Up Connections*, then the *Advanced* menu; choose the *Dial-Up Preferences* box we talked about earlier and select the *Callback* tab.

B. After you're connected, you can choose whether you will have the option of entering a callback number. If you indicate that you want to be called, the RAS will end the call and call you back. Your modem will be set to answer the next incoming call, the authentication process will repeat, and then you'll be on the remote network.

4. Tips for accessing remote resources by modem:

A. Run application software from your own local computer. Applications accessed remotely take a long time to run.

B. Tell Windows to redial as we discussed earlier in the event that you get disconnected.

C. Place shortcuts on the desktop for dial-up connections that are used often.

D. Drag a copy of a remote file to your local desktop. Work on it, and drag it back when you're finished.

Part 3 Disconnect from Remote Network

1. Right-click the Dial-Up Networking icon on the Taskbar and click Disconnect.

2. Place the lab in your journal.

Routing and Remote Access Service (RRAS)

LAB **17.1**

■ INTRODUCTION

The purpose of this lab is to introduce you to the service on Windows 2000 Server that provides connectivity and management of remote access connections. Other server operating systems can provide similar services, but we will only explore the particular services of Windows 2000 Server in this lab. Routing and Remote Access Service and Network and Dial-Up Connections are tools used to install, configure, and provide access management to Windows 2000 Server. You can use Network and Dial-Up Connections to connect a Windows 2000 Server to another computer, a private network, or the Internet.

We will use the tools provided with Windows 2000 Server and establish an outgoing connection with a remote computer. We will also explore one or two methods of allowing remote computers to connect to our server. This lab only provides an introduction to a part of the services offered by Windows 2000 Server. It is beyond the scope of this book to provide all the information about the services provided by this or any other operating system.

■ WHAT YOU WILL DO

- Install and configure RRAS
- Configure an inbound dial-up connection
- Configure an outbound dial-up connection

■ WHAT YOU WILL NEED

- Computer with Windows 2000 Server operating system
- Installed NICs, modems, COM ports, etc. used for the remote connection
- Connectivity to the Internet or a private network

■ SETTING UP

Part 1 Install and Configure RRAS

1. Access the various components of the communication devices through Device Manager. Click *Start > Settings > Control Panel >* System. Choose the tab labeled *Hardware* and select *Device Manager*.

2. The properties of a particular device are revealed by right-clicking on the device. Make sure that all the COM ports, modems, network adapters, and so on are installed properly. The network protocol used for each device will have to be configured, but first we must activate RRAS. RRAS is installed by default, but is not activated by default.

3. *Click Start > Programs > Administrative Tools > Routing and Remote Access.* Choose which RRAS server you want to activate.

4. After the server is selected, a server setup wizard will appear.

5. Choices can be made from the list of common configurations including *Internet connection server, Remote access server, VPN server, Network router*, and *Manually configured server*.

6. After choosing which configuration option you want, the wizard states that the service you checked is configured and is either ready for immediate use or ready for further configuration, depending on the service selected.

7. Click *Finish* on the wizard.

Part 2 Configure an Inbound Dial-Up Connection

1. The RRAS is capable of permitting many different types of inbound connections. We'll focus on just one type: modem ports.

2. Click *Start > Programs > Administrative Tools > Routing and Remote Access*.

3. Select Ports under the name of the server to which you are configuring access. Right-click *Ports*, which pops up the *Ports Properties* box. Note the Standard 56000bps v.90 modem.

4. Highlight the modem and choose *Configure* to open the modem dialog box. You can then select *Remote access connections* (inbound only) and provide the phone number to use. Now remote access inbound connections are enabled.

Part 3 Configure an Outbound Dial-Up Connection

1. Choose *Start > Settings > Network and Dial-Up Connections* tab. Double-click the *Make New Connection* icon to open the connection wizard.

2. Click *Next* to continue with the wizard. Select the *Dial up to private network* button and click *Next*.

3. A dialog box will appear where you will choose the phone number dialed and the dialing rules you need to use, for example, *70.

4. The *Connection Availability* box defines which users can use the connection.

5. Click *Next*. Internet Connection Sharing enables other users of the network to access these connection resources. Decide also whether to enable on-demand dialing. This feature allows a connection to be made automatically when a computer on the network tries to access external resources. (If you enable this feature, your computer will have to use the 192.168.0.1 address.)

6. Choose *Next* and the *Completing the Network Connection Wizard* dialog box pops up. Here you can name the connection that you've just created and add a shortcut on the desktop. You should be all set to dial an outbound connection.

7. Place the lab in your journal.

Dynamic Host Configuration Protocol (DHCP)

LAB 17.2

■ INTRODUCTION

TCP/IP configuration on computers can be accomplished by either manually entering static IP addresses or automatically providing dynamic addresses. Managing a large number of devices can be a time-consuming task. DHCP can provide a means to manage the addressing scheme of any size network. The DHCP service can be run on a Windows 2000 server, providing addresses to many different client operating systems.

Network information is provided to the DHCP clients, including the IP address, subnet mask, default gateways, addresses of DNS servers, WINS server address, and DHCP lease information. A pool of addresses assignable to DHCP clients is defined on the DHCP server. The client computers must have their network settings configured to request an IP address from the DHCP server.

A DHCP lease is accomplished in four steps. The acronym used to remember the process is DORA.

- *Discover*: This is where the client computer broadcasts a dhcpdiscover searching for a DHCP server. The client MAC address, computer name, DHCP options supported, and a message ID are sent to the server.
- *Offer*: The DHCP server receives the discover message and determines if the request is valid. If it is valid, the DHCP server sends a dhcpoffer message to the client MAC address with an IP address that is available for a lease along with parameters relating to length of the lease. This message is a broadcast message. If more than one DHCP server is on the network, all of them respond to the discover message and offer an IP address.
- *Request*: The DHCP client takes the dhcpoffer and accepts the IP address that is offered. It then sends a dhcprequest to all the DHCP servers that responded to its discover message with the message that it has accepted a particular offer. This way all the DHCP servers that offered an IP address that was not taken can use the address for another offer.
- *Acknowledge*: The DHCP server that made the offer that was accepted notifies the client with an acknowledgment broadcast called a dhcpack. The client can then finish its TCP/IP setup with the information given by the DHCP server. If a request fails for any reason, the server broadcasts a dhcpnack message and the client computer starts the DHCP process again.

The DHCP-provided IP address is leased to the client for a default time of eight days. This lease time can be changed. Halfway through the lease, the client computer will attempt to renew its lease. The client computer, generally speaking, will try to keep the same IP address even when it is shut down. You can release and renew the IP address with an IPCONFIG/RELEASE and an IPCONFIG/RENEW command to see that the server will usually assign the same IP address to the client.

■ WHAT YOU WILL DO

- Install and configure DHCP

■ WHAT YOU WILL NEED

- Computer with Windows 2000 Server installed
- Connection to a LAN

■ SETTING UP

Part I Windows 2000 Server DHCP Configuration

1. DHCP service provision requires that the server be configured with the following:
   A. Static IP address
   B. Subnet mask
   C. Default gateway
   D. DHCP service installed
   E. Range of IP addresses to lease
   F. Authorization with Active Directory services

2. DHCP servers must have at least one scope (range of IP addresses to use).
   A. Addresses in separate scopes cannot overlap.
   B. Statically assigned IP addresses must be removed from the scope.

Part 2 Installation and Configuration of a DHCP Scope

1. The server configuration steps outlined in Part 1 must be completed first.
   A. Use 10.0.1.250 and the subnet mask of 255.255.255.0 and statically assign it to the server.
   B. We'll use a scope (range of addresses used) of 10.0.1.10–10.0.1.200.
   C. The addresses we'll exclude from the scope are 10.0.1.1–10.0.1.9.
   D. The default gateway should be set at 10.0.1.254.

2. Open *Control Panel*.

3. Click *Add/Remove Programs*.

4. Click *Add/Remove Windows Components*.

5. Choose *Networking Services > Details*. Check the box next to *Dynamic Host Configuration Protocol (DHCP)* and click *OK*.

6. Click *Next*. You might have to put the Windows 2000 Server disk in at this point.

7. When the Install process is done, click *Finish* on the wizard.

8. Click *Start > Programs > Administrative Tools > DHCP* to start the DHCP manager.

9. Double-click the server in the left pane.

10. Right-click the server name and click on *New Scope*.

11. The *New Scope Wizard* will launch. Click *Next*.

12. Enter a name for the scope like ADDRESS1. Click *Next*.

13. Put in the address range of the scope, start IP address 10.0.1.10 and end IP address 10.0.1.200. Define the subnet mask as 24 bits or 255.255.255.0. Click *Next*.

14. Enter the IP addresses that will be excluded, start IP address 10.0.1.1 and end IP address 10.0.1.9. Click *Next*.

15. Clicking *Next* will now accept the default lease time of 8 days.

16. Click *Next* to choose DHCP options.

17. Enter the default gateway 10.0.1.254 in the field provided and click *Add*.

18. Skip DNS and WINS configuration for now by clicking *Next*.

19. Click *Next* to activate the scope.

20. Click *Finish* to complete the *New Scope Wizard*.

21. Now right-click the server and select *Authorize* from the menu.

22. The DHCP server should now indicate a Scope that is "Active".

23. Close the DHCP manager.

24. Configure a client machine to obtain an address from a DHCP server and confirm that the activated service will work.

25. Place the lab in your journal.

Domain Name System (DNS)

LAB **17.3**

■ INTRODUCTION

Domain Name System is used to provide name-to-address translations in an Internet-based network. DNS names are ordered in a hierarchical structure with the top-level domain consisting of major address groups called .com, .gov, .org, .edu, .net, and others. The second-level domains are those like apple.com or fbi.gov. The second-level domains can be subdivided further to identify a specific computer. The Internet name *www.stny.rr.com* identifies a Web server named www in the stny subdomain of the rr subdomain of the .com domain. The path to the server is found by traveling up the hierarchical structure from the .com up to the www server.

We will install and configure Domain Name System on a Windows 200 Server to provide DNS service to our network.

■ WHAT YOU WILL DO

- Install and configure Domain Name System services

■ WHAT YOU WILL NEED

- Computer with Windows 2000 Server installed
- A LAN

■ SETTING UP

Install and Configure Domain Name System

1. Guidelines for creating domain names:
   A. The names assigned to each object in a domain must be unique.
   B. The maximum number of characters in a Fully Qualified Domain Name (FQDN) is 63, but make it shorter than that. After all, how many letters are you willing to type to access a domain name?
   C. The number of subdomains should be less than four to reduce the number of steps required to resolve a name and to make it easier for someone to remember the name.
   D. Characters that can be used to define a domain name include a–z, A–Z, 0–9, and the hyphen -.

   2. Zones of Authority must be established with one name server in authority to map names for the zone. A zone can be further divided into many zones, each with its own authority. A large network will typically have more than one DNS server to handle DNS requests.

3. When a DNS server is created, the "Start of Authority" (SOA) and "Name Server" (NS) resource records are added automatically. The SOA record identifies the address of the name server in authority for the specific zone. NS records state the addresses of name servers of specific domains. If a server cannot handle a DNS request locally, it is instructed how to handle the request according to these two records.

4. Installation of DNS.

   A. Open *Control Panel*.
   B. Click *Add/Remove Programs*.
   C. Click *Add/Remove Windows Components*.
   D. Select *Networking Services > Details*.
   E. Click the box next to *Domain Name System (DNS)*.
   F. Click *Next* to install DNS. The Windows 2000 Server disk might be needed.
   G. Click *Finish* to close the *Install Wizard*.
   H. For the configuration of DNS:

      i. Click *Start > Programs > Administrative Tools > DNS* to open the DNS manager.
      ii. Choose your server from the left pane and choose *Configure the Server* by right-clicking the icon.
      iii. Click *Next* to start the wizard.
      iv. Click *Next* to create a forward lookup zone.
      v. On the next page choose the *Active Directory Integrated* button and *Next*.
      vi. Enter **rr.com** for the zone name and click *Next*.
      vii. Click *Next* to create a reverse lookup zone.
      viii. Click the *Network ID* and put 10.0.1 in the blank. This follows the same addressing context as that of the lab on DHCP. Click *Next*.
      ix. Click *Finish*.
      x. On the left pane of the DNS manager, double-click the server and double-click each zone.
      xi. Open *Properties* in the forward lookup zone rr.com and click the *General* tab. In the *Allow dynamic updates?* box specify *Only Secure Updates*.
      xii. Test your DNS configuration by specifying the DNS server on a local client machine as the only DNS option and attempt to browse a known Web site.

5. Place the lab in your journal.

Linux DNS Service

■ INTRODUCTION

DNS servers provide name to IP address resolution so that the Fully Qualified Domain Name (FQDN) may be used to connect to a local or remote site instead of having to remember and type an IP address. I think everyone would agree that a domain name is easier to remember than an IP address.

There are three basic types of domain servers: primary, secondary, and caching. A primary DNS server is the authoritative server for a particular domain. The secondary DNS server works as a backup or support server to the primary. Caching servers don't store configuration files for a domain but simply cache DNS requests for future use.

The option to install a DNS server is provided when the Linux Red Hat operating system is installed. BIND is still the DNS server of choice for most Linux servers.

After the DNS server is installed on the network the various client computers must be provided certain information related to this service. For a computer user who connects to the Internet with an ISP, the ISP usually provides this service. The domain name entered would reflect the domain name that the ISP provided. If the computer user is connected to a domain created for a group of users associated with a business or school, the primary, secondary, and caching DNS servers would normally provide DNS service to the network. For the purposes of this lab we assume that DNS service is provided by an ISP and note that the IP addresses we will use for examples are actually private addresses (not routable on the Internet).

■ WHAT YOU WILL DO

- Determine addresses of DNS server, SMTP server, and POP server
- Configure DNS services on a client computer

■ WHAT YOU WILL NEED

- Computer with Linux operating system installed
- NIC or modem installed and Internet connectivity established

■ SETTING UP

Part I Determine Addresses of DNS Server

1. ISP provided the IP addresses of the DNS servers in its domain called NET+.

2. The addresses of the three DNS servers are: 192.168.1.254, 192.168.2.254, and 192.168.3.254.

Part 2 Configure DNS Services on Client Computers

1. Start *linuxconf.*

2. Choose *Config > Networking > Client Tasks > Name Server Specifications.*

3. Check the box that says "DNS is required for normal operation".

4. Enter the domain name **NET+.com** in the box that specifies the default domain.

5. Enter the addresses of the three DNS servers that were provided by the ISP in the boxes for nameserver 1, nameserver 2, and nameserver 3.

6. Place the lab in your journal.

Linux NIC Setup

LAB **18.2**

■ INTRODUCTION

The NIC must be configured if your Linux machine is to be connected to a LAN. Red Hat installation detects most NICs during the installation process and will automatically set up most of the parameters related to networking with a Linux machine. You will have to provide some information in order for the process to be completed.

An IP address is the first thing you will need. We can either set the IP address statically or obtain one through the use of DHCP or BOOTP when the computer is booted. Obviously the network must have a DHCP or BOOTP server running for these services if we are to use them. Ask your system administrator what type of IP address should be used.

If our network connection is to an ISP, the IP address is provided from a pool of addresses the ISP owns or from a private addressing scheme the ISP uses and translates to "real" IP addresses before the traffic hits the Internet.

A subnet mask is also required for the network configuration. A novice networker should at least know that the subnet mask for class A networks is 255.0.0.0, for class B networks is 255.255.0.0, and for class C networks is 255.255.255.0. This is the classful approach to networking. The advanced Network+ candidate should also understand that Classless Inter Domain Routing (CIDR) provides the methods for subnetting each of these various IP address classes.

The name of your machine and the name of your domain are also needed to complete the configuration. Give your machine a name that is easy to remember. If your machine is under the administration of someone else you will not have this option.

■ WHAT YOU WILL DO

- Configure a NIC on a Linux machine
- Test the configuration

■ WHAT YOU WILL NEED

- Computer with Linux operating system
- NIC installed
- Network connectivity to other computers

■ SETTING UP

Part I Configure a NIC on a Linux Machine

1. Choose *Config > Networking > Client tasks*.
2. Select *Basic host information* in the *linuxconf* program.

3. Click on *Adaptor 1* for the first Ethernet Adapter Card (NIC).

4. Manually enter the IP address. We'll use 10.0.0.1 for this network.

5. Enter the subnet mask of **255.0.0.0**.

6. The domain name, kernel module, and net device are all configurable parameters that are normally entered along with the IP address and mask during the initial installation of the operating system.

Part 2 Test the Configuration

1. The status of the IP address configuration can be checked with the /sbin/ifconfig -a command. The reflected output should show the 10.0.0.1 address with a 255.0.0.0 mask under the configuration parameters for eth0.

2. Use the ping utility to test connectivity with another computer on the network. The IP address and mask must be compatible with the one used on this machine. (The addresses 10.0.0.2–10.255.255.254 could be used.)

3. Place the lab in your journal.

Linux Network Testing

LAB **18.3**

■ INTRODUCTION

Testing should be done on a network as each computer connection is established. A list of the available IP addresses on the network should be available. The KDE desktop environment provides a network utilities program called knu (KDE network utilities) that provides the ping, traceroute, DNS, finger, and mtr utilities in one application. Network testing utilities can also be run from the command prompt and are useful for determining connectivity and network bottlenecks. The purpose of this lab is to acquaint you with a few of the network utilities that are part of the Linux Red Hat operating system package.

Ping is a program used to test network connectivity. It sends a group of small messages to a remote computer and waits for a response to those messages. If the messages don't return, a problem is indicated on either your local computer, the remote computer, or the network between the two. A ping can be attempted to a hostname or to a specific IP address. Keep in mind that pinging to a hostname may not indicate the failure of the network but only a failure of DNS. A message indicating that the hostname is unknown may indicate a DNS failure.

The traceroute utility works in a similar fashion to a ping except that it records the output of the path one hop at a time. Each network segment that the packet traverses and the time each hop takes are recorded in the output of the traceroute command. This will assist the network administrator in determining the location of bottlenecks.

■ WHAT YOU WILL DO

- Ping a remote computer
- Trace a route to a remote computer

■ WHAT YOU WILL NEED

- Computer with Linux Red Hat operating system installed
- Connection to a LAN or to the Internet

■ SETTING UP

Part I Ping a Remote Computer

1. The syntax for a ping command is: *$ ping (hostname or IP address)*
2. The Linux-generated ping will continue forever by default. Ctrl+C will stop it.
3. An example of the command and the response is as follows:

```
$ Ping www.sunnybroome.edu
PING www.sunnybroome.edu (192.203.130.2) : 56 data bytes
```

```
64 bytes from 192.203.130.2: icmp_seq = 0 ttl = 64 time = 0.4 ms
64 bytes from 192.203.130.2: icmp_seq = 1 ttl = 64 time = 0.4 ms
```

Ctrl+C is pressed to stop the ping and the response is:

```
--overkill.globalmt.com ping statistics -
2 packets transmitted, 2 packets received, 0% packet loss
round-trip min/avg/max = 0.4/0.4/0.4 ms
```

4. The ping command could have been entered as:

```
$ ping 192.203.130.2
```

and the response would have been very similar:

```
PING 192.203.130.2 : 56 data bytes
64 bytes from 192.203.130.2: icmp_seq = 0 ttl = 64 time = 0.4 ms
64 bytes from 192.203.130.2: icmp_seq = 1 ttl = 64 time = 0.4 ms
```

5. Remember that the ping utility can also be accessed through the KDE desktop environment.

6. A ping failure would look like this:

```
$ ping 192.203.130.2
Ping 192.203.130.2 : 56 data bytes
```

Ctrl+C...to stop the ping

```
192.203.130.2 ping statistics
20 packets transmitted, 0 packets received, 100% packet loss
```

Part 2 Traceroute to a Remote Computer

1. The traceroute command can be used to trace each specific hop that packets take on their way to a prescribed destination.

2. An example of the command and the response is as follows:

```
$ /usr/sbin/traceroute www.yahoo.com
1  bing100b.stny.lrun.com [204.210.132.1] 26.49 ms 36.445 ms
30.16 ms
2  m2.stny.lrun.com [204.210.159.17] 10.113 ms  14.451 ms
9.132 ms
3  ext_router.stny.lrun.com [204.210.155.18] 26.49 ms 36.445
ms 30.16 ms
4  border3-serial4-0-6.Greensboro.mci.net [204.70.83.85]
26.49 ms 36.445 ms 30.16  ms
5  core1-fddi-0.Greensboro.mci.net [204.70.80.17] 37.307 ms
¬55.862 ms 39.374 ms
6  bordercore2.Bloomington.mci.net [166.48.176.1] 109.22 ms
160.11 ms  122.13 ms
7  hssi1-0.br2.NUQ.globalcenter.net [166.48.177.254] 123.366
ms  126.399 ms  113.111 ms
8  fe5-1.cr1.NUQ.globalcenter.net [206.251.1.33] 37.307 ms
¬55.862 ms 39.374 ms
9  pos0-0.wr1.NUQ.globalcenter.net [206.251.0.122] 114.165
ms  125.855 ms  113.121 ms
```

```
10  pos1-0-OC12.wr1.SNV.globalcenter.net [206.251.0.74]
37.307 ms 55.862 ms 39.374 ms

11  pos5-0.cr1.SNV.globalcenter.net [206.251.0.105] 55.806 ms
62.596 ms  56.182 ms

12  www7.yahoo.com [204.71.200.72] 40.371 ms * 41.389 ms
```

3. Place the lab in your journal.

The following information relating to the ping and traceroute commands was downloaded from the following Web site: *http://www.computerhope.com/unix/utracero.htm*

Syntax for ping Command

```
ping -s [-d] [-l] [-L] [-n] [-r] [-R] [-v] [ -i interface_
address ] [-I interval] [-t ttl] host [packetsize] [count]
```

```
-d Set the SO_DEBUG socket option.
-l Loose source route. Use this option in the IP header to
send the packet to the given host and back again. Usually
specified with the -R option.
-L Turn off loopback of multicast packets. Normally, if
there are members in the host group on the outgoing inter-
face, a copy of the multicast packets will be delivered to
the local machine.
-n Show network addresses as numbers. ping normally displays
addresses as host names.
-r Bypass the normal routing tables and send directly to a
host on an attached network. If the host is not on a
directly-attached network, an error is returned. This option
can be used to ping a local host through an interface that
has been dropped by the router daemon.
-R Record route. Sets the IP record route option, which will
store the route of the packet inside the IP header. The con-
tents of the record route will only be printed if the -v
option is given, and only be set on return packets if the
target host preserves the record route option across echos,
or the -l option is given.
-v Verbose output. List any ICMP packets, other than
ECHO_RESPONSE, that are received.
-i interface_address Specify the outgoing interface address
to use for multicast packets. The default interface address
for multicast packets is determined from the (unicast) rout-
ing tables.
-I interval Specify the interval between successive trans-
missions. The default is one second.
-t ttl Specify the IP time to live for unicast and multicast
packets. The default time to live for unicast packets is set
with ndd (using the icmp_def_ttl variable). The default time
to live for multicast is one hop.
host The network host.
packetsize Specified size of packetsize. Default is 64.
count Amount of times to send the ping request.
```

Syntax for traceroute Command

```
traceroute [-d] [-F] [-I] [-n] [-v] [-x] [-f first_ttl] [-g
gateway [-g gateway] | -r] [-i iface] [-m max_ttl] [-p port]
[-q nqueries] [-s src_addr] [-t tos] [-w waittime ] host
[packetlen]
```

-d Set the SO_DEBUG socket option.

-F Set the "don't fragment" bit.

-I Use ICMP ECHO instead of UDP datagrams.

-n Print hop addresses numerically rather than symbolically and numerically. This saves a nameserver address-to-name lookup for each gateway found on the path.

-v Verbose output. For each hop, the size and the destination of the response packets is displayed. Also ICMP packets received other than TIME_EXCEEDED and UNREACHABLE are listed as well.

-x Prevent traceroute from calculating checksums. Note that checksums are usually required for the last hop when using ICMP ECHO probes. See the -I option.

-f first_ttl Set the starting ttl value to first_ttl, to override the default value 1. traceroute skips processing for those intermediate gateways which are less than first_ttl hops away.

-g gateway Specify a loose source route gateway. The user can specify more than one gateway by using -g for each gateway. The maximum that can be set is 8.

-r Bypass the normal routing tables and send directly to a host on an attached network. If the host is not on a directly-attached network, an error is returned. This option can be used to send probes to a local host through an interface that has been dropped by the router daemon.

-i iface Specify a network interface to obtain the source IP address for outgoing probe packets. This is normally only useful on a multi-homed host. The -s option is also another way to do this. Note that this option does not provide a way to specify the interface on which the probe packets are sent.

-m max_ttl Set the maximum ttl used in outgoing probe packets. The default is 30 hops, which is the same default used for TCP connections.

-p port Set the base UDP port number used in probes. The default is 33434. traceroute hopes that nothing is listening on UDP ports (base+(nhops- 1)*nqueries) to (base+(nhops* nqueries)-1)at the destination host, so that an ICMP PORT_UNREACHABLE message will be returned to terminate the route tracing. If something is listening on a port in the default range, this option can be used to select an unused port range. nhops is defined as the number of hops between the source and the destination.

-q nqueries Set the desired number of probe queries. The default is 3.

-s src_addr Use the following address, which usually is given as an IP address, not a hostname, as the source address in outgoing probe packets. On multi-homed hosts, those with more than one IP address, this option can be used to force the source address to be something other than the IP address traceroute picks by default. If the IP address is not one of this machine's interface addresses, an error is returned and nothing is sent. When used together with the -i option, the given IP address should be configured on the specified interface. Otherwise, an error will be returned.

-t tos Set the tos(type-of-service) in probe packets to the specified value. The default is zero. The value must be an integer in the range from 0 to 255. Gateways along the path may route the probe packet differently depending upon the tos value set in the probe packet.

-w waittime Set the time, in seconds, to wait for a response to a probe. The default is five (5) seconds.

host The network host.

Mac OS X Networking

LAB 19.1

■ INTRODUCTION

The Mac OS X operating system comes equipped to network using TCP/IP as well as AppleTalk using the Network System Preference window. All the network settings are managed in this window. Most of the settings and information related to Network System Preference are normally entered using the Setup Assistant right after the operating system is installed.

The "Locations" drop down box on the Network System Preference page enables the user to choose between location configurations, create new ones, or edit the ones that already exist. One "Automatic" configuration is already defined including all the devices detected by the operating system that are configured to use DHCP. Clicking on the "Show" menu allows the selection of individual active devices. Tabs are revealed below the menu according to the selection made. The "Active Network Ports" information is shown in the lower part of the Network System Preference window. Active ports are shown with checked boxes. The Lock button can be clicked to prevent further changes.

Keep in mind that if you set up the network connections manually (no DHCP or BOOTP used to automate connections) an IP address and a subnet mask that agree with the configuration of the other devices on the network must be selected.

In addition to the TCP/IP tab, a PPPoE tab is available for DSL Internet connections or for wireless AirPort connections. Your ISP should be consulted for these particular settings. An AppleTalk tab is available for the connections to your AppleTalk network. This configuration can be done automatically. A Proxies tab is available for proxy server selection for various Internet protocols. Proxy servers are used to improve security and performance, or to filter information.

In this lab we'll configure the Mac OS X computer with the basics to get it started on the network. We'll assume that the network you connect to uses the services of a DHCP server.

■ WHAT YOU WILL DO

- Configure networking on a Mac OS X machine

■ WHAT YOU WILL NEED

- A computer with Mac OS X operating system installed
- Connection to a network with a DHCP server

■ SETTING UP

Configure Networking on a Mac

1. Open *System Preferences* from the Dock.

2. Double-click on *Network*.

3. A *Network* box like the one shown below will appear.

4. Built-in Ethernet will be the option that comes up if the computer is connected to an Ethernet.

5. Choose *Configure Using DHCP* and the needed information will be entered by the DHCP server.

6. Click the *Show All* icon in the top left corner of the window.

7. A window will appear asking if you want to save the configuration changes. Click the *Save* option.

8. Now you are ready to participate in the network.

9. Place the lab in your journal.

Mac OS X to Windows XP Networking

LAB **19.2**

■ INTRODUCTION

The purpose of this lab is to provide the methods to connect the Mac OS X computer with a Windows computer. The easiest way to accomplish this is to set up the Mac computer as a client on the Windows network. This is accomplished by enabling file sharing on the Windows computer. The method used to connect to Windows operating systems other than the XP system will be different, but the basic tasks to connect will be similar.

■ WHAT YOU WILL DO

• Connect a Mac OS X computer to a Windows XP computer

■ WHAT YOU WILL NEED

• One computer with Mac OS X
• One computer with Windows XP
• Hub and two straight cables

■ SETTING UP

Connect a Mac OS X to a Windows XP

1. On the Windows XP machine, right-click on the drive that you want to share. Click on the *Sharing and Security* option.

2. Click on the *Sharing* tab in the page that opens.

3. Check the box that shares this folder on the network and decide whether to allow network users to change your files.

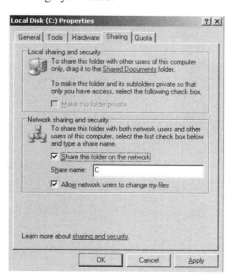

4. On the Mac machine, click on the desktop to activate the *Finder*, choose *Go*, and choose the *Connect to Server*, option.

5. The Windows computer will show up as one of the available network servers. After the account data is entered, the Windows drive will appear on the Mac Desktop like any of the other available drives.

6. There are other ways to accomplish this networking interaction. An Internet search of Mac OS X networking is sure to reveal additional methods.

7. Place the lab in your journal.

Mac OS X E-Mail

■ INTRODUCTION

The Mac OS X provides e-mail service among its many features. Various settings are required to enable this service. The purpose of this lab is to lead you through the necessary steps required to set up the e-mail service on your Mac computer.

■ WHAT YOU WILL DO

• Set up the e-mail service

■ WHAT YOU WILL NEED

• Computer with Mac OS X

■ SETTING UP

Set Up E-Mail Service

1. Open *Mail* from the desktop or the hard drive and click on *Preferences*.

2. Select *Add Account*.

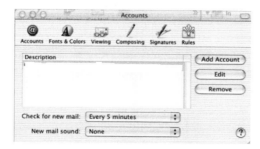

3. For the *Account Type* choose *POP*.

4. Enter your e-mail address in the *Description* box and again in the Email Address box.

5. Enter your name in the *Full Name* box.

6. In the *Incoming Mail Server* box, enter the address of your mail server.

7. Enter your login name in the *User Name* box.

8. Enter a password in the *Password* box.

9. Click on *Options*.

10. In the *Outgoing Mail Server* box enter the address of the SMTP server.

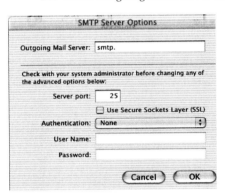

11. Click *OK* without a *User Name* and *Password* unless instructed otherwise by your ISP.

12. The box shown above will now appear except that all the pertinent information would be included in the blank boxes shown.

13. Place the lab in your journal.